AF326620

THE NAKED **TRUTH** ABOUT NUDISM

By the same author

Naked and Unashamed: Nudism from Six Points of View

It's Only Natural: The Philosophy of Nudism

available from
wolfbaitbooks.com

First published in 1935
This edition published in 2024
by Wolfbait Books
www.wolfbait.co.uk

A CIP record for this book is available from the British Library
ISBN: 978-1-917298-04-9 (hardback)
ISBN: 978-1-917298-05-6 (ebook)

THE NAKED TRUTH ABOUT NUDISM

By William Welby

Foreword by Brian Curragh, MA

Photographs by Stephen Glass

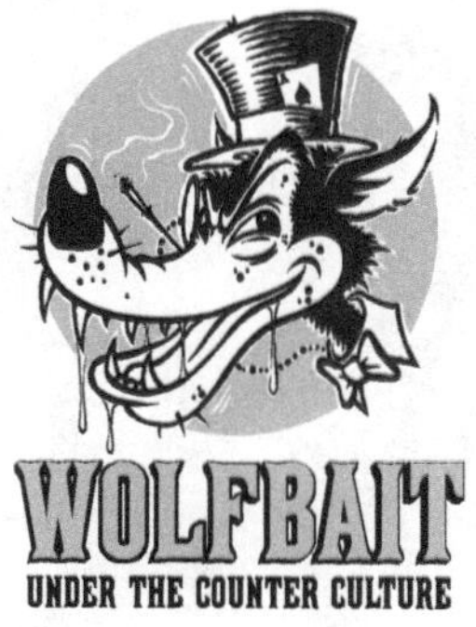

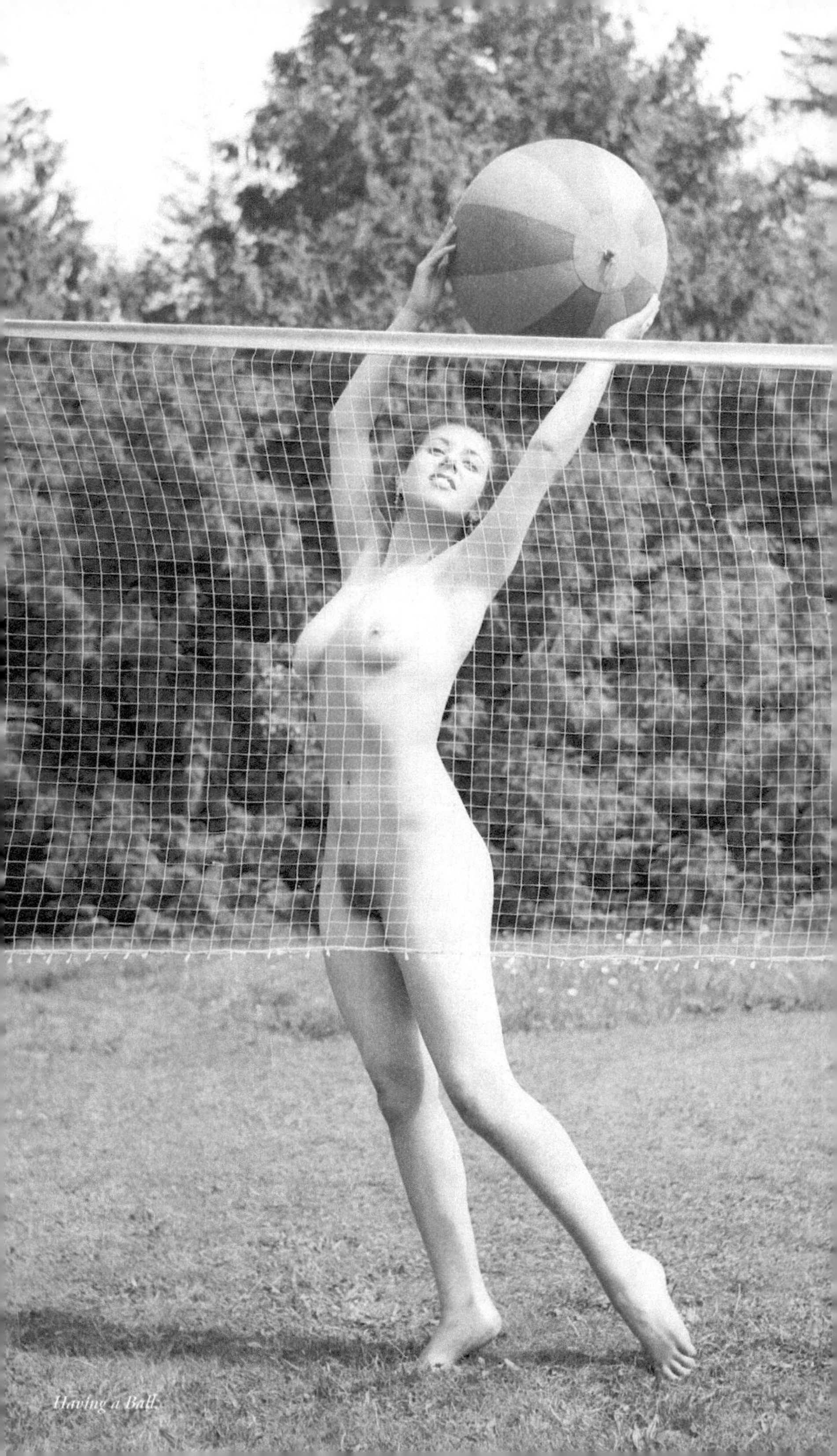

Having a Ball.

Contents

Illustrations
by Stephen Glass

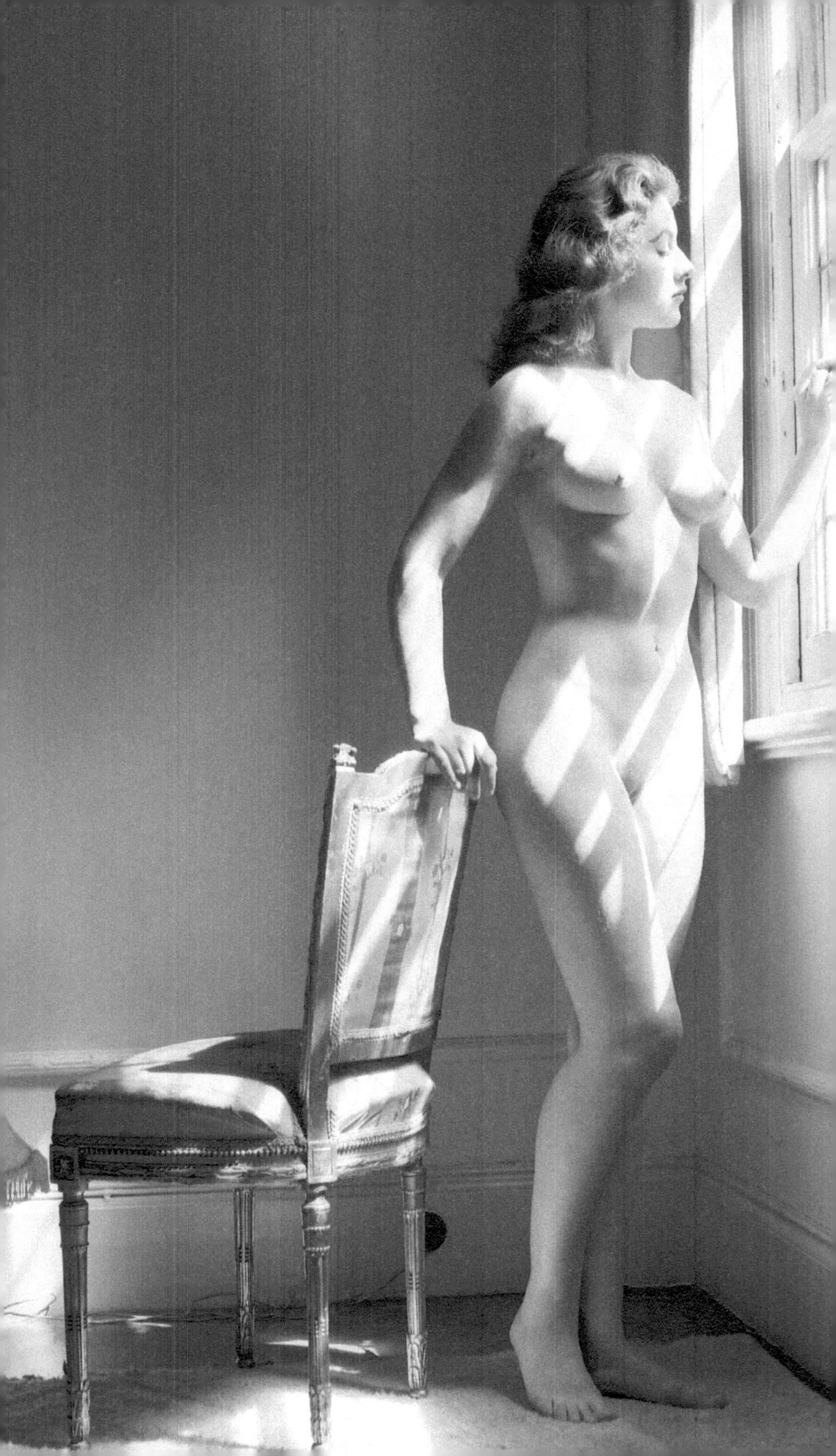

Foreword

WHO WAS WILLIAM WELBY? Actually, let's step back briefly and deal with who he wasn't. He wasn't Rex Wellbye, as some had considered a possibility.

Rex Wellbye – or to give him his birth name, Reginald Wellbye – is a well-known figure in the history of naturism in Great Britain. Together with Harold Booth and Mark Sorensen, he founded the English Gymnosophy Society in 1922 and was an original member of the mysterious Moonella Group, which practised sunbathing in a field near Wickford, Essex, over the summers of 1924 and 1925. All members of the group used club names to protect their identity – Rex Wellbye's was "Zex". In 1927, Wellbye acquired some land which became the Fouracres Club; it continues today as the Fiveacres Country Club, making it the oldest surviving naturist club in the UK. Outside of naturism, Wellbye earned a living by writing topographical touring guides to England for the motorist and cyclist.

So, when the phonetically identical William Welby published three books on nudism between 1934 and 1937, the suspicion arose that he and Wellbye were one and the same person. However, a review of the UK Births, Marriages and Death registers, alongside census returns, reveals that Reginald Wellbye was born on the 6th April 1873 in Marylebone, London, to parents Henry Read Wellbeloved/Wellbye and Helen Brooks, while William Welby arrived almost ten years

---

Left: *Sun-kissed.*

later, on 1st April 1883 in Canterbury, Kent, to parents George Welby and his second wife, Mary Jane Durant. The two men can be tracked down through the years until William Welby's death, aged 68, on 14th May 1951 at his home on Hainault Road, Chigwell, Essex. Reginald Wellbye lived on to the age of 89, dying in the first quarter of 1963, reportedly at the Fiveacres Club he had founded.

So, these were two different men who both played important roles in enabling the practice of naturism in Great Britain.

While Rex Wellbye's contribution was towards the physical creation of naturist clubs, William Welby's three books were among the first to bring the concepts behind nudism/naturism to the attention of the wider British public.

Having worked initially as an auctioneer's clerk in London and then as an advertising copywriter, by 1921 Welby was employed as the advertising manager for Achille Serre Ltd, the company which introduced dry cleaning to the UK, and was working at their head office in Hackney Wick. By 1929, he had become an associate director and publicity manager there.

What exactly happened in Welby's life over the next five years is lost to history, but we do know that in July 1934 he wrote his first book on nudism: *Naked and Unashamed: Nudism from Six Points of View.* It is quite possible that *Naked and Unashamed* was the second book published in England on nudism after Rev. C.E. Norwood's 1933 *Nudism in England.* The book is an introduction to nudism seen from six "points of view", and covers the history of nudism, the moral, health and psychological aspects of the practice, the aesthetic considerations, and the "Commonsense Point of View". What is clear from the first edition is that Welby was an external observer of nudism as it rapidly developed in Britain in the 1930s. His motives may well have been commercial, in a manner similar to George Ryley Scott's *The Commonsense of Nudism*, also published in 1934.

The following year, 1935, Welby wrote this volume, *The Naked Truth about Nudism*, and while the Author's Preface initially sheds little further light on Welby's personal experiences, by Chapter V, he admits that following "the remarkable success" of *Naked and Unashamed*, he had received "invitations to visit various Nudist clubs, and after my first real experience, I became an enthusiastic Nudist myself".

What this means is that *The Naked Truth* is written from a much more personal point of view and conviction. It suggests that Welby was rather more than the detached observer he portrayed himself as in *Naked and Unashamed*. He admits that before writing the first volume, he had "studied the subject very closely from all angles. I read practically everything that was printed about the subject and supplemented my reading with personal enquiries wherever and whenever possible." The publication of *Naked and Unashamed* brought him the opportunity to visit some of the early British nudist clubs and this experience enabled him to fill his second book with many personal, albeit anonymous, accounts directly from the members of those clubs, thereby making this a fascinating historical review of nudism in Britain in the 1930s.

The Naked Truth about Nudism assumes that the reader may not be familiar with the practice, so it introduces it and looks at the health benefits and the social opportunities it can bring before dealing with the thorny issue of nudity and sex. In a

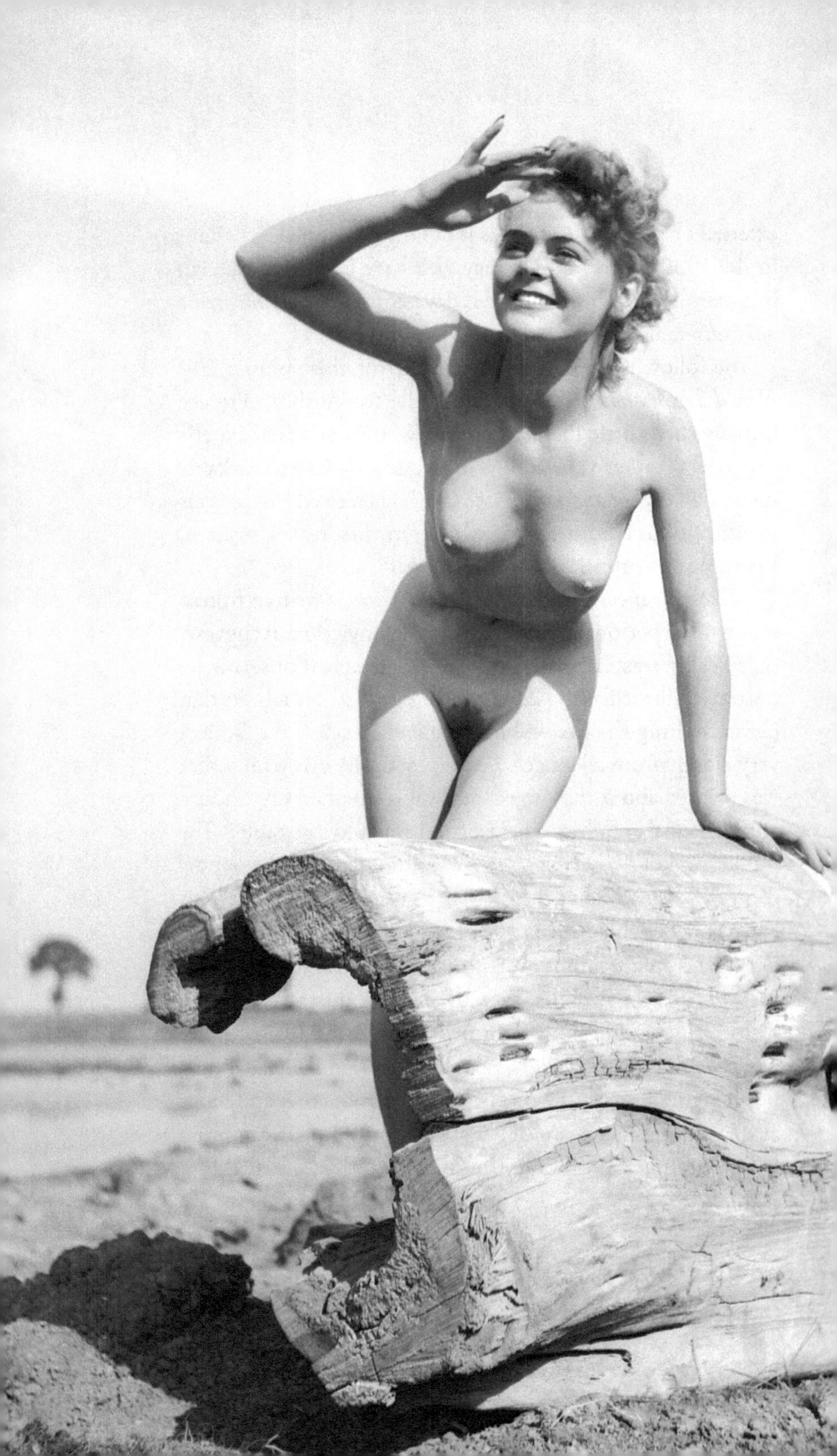

chapter entitled "Subordination of Sex" Welby sets out his reasoning that:

> ... the practice of nudism is beneficial. Mere physical attributes partially revealed will cease to excite curiosity, and a train of thought leading to eroticism once the whole of the body has become familiar by sight. For these reasons Nudism does subordinate sex without in any sense repressing it, and by so doing is favourable to health, psychologically as well as physically.

The following two chapters explore why people became nudists, through interviews with several club members, and then offer an excellent account of Welby's visits to many of the early clubs, including the New Forest Club, the Lotus League of North Finchley, Yew Tree Camp and the White House, before Mr & Mrs Welby and family became members of a nudist club in their home county of Essex. Welby also sets out the ideal operating practices that anyone considering opening a nudist club should follow.

Welby brings the book to a conclusion by looking at Artificial Sunlight and "Indoor" Nudism before setting out his expectations for the future of nudism. He expresses regret for the many "adherents of Nudism who, for professional and material reasons, are reluctant to make their opinions public" and states that personally, he has "not the least objection to anyone knowing I am a Nudist and that I and my wife and family enjoy healthy exercise and interesting companionship

Left: *Bright Horizon.*

at a Nudist camp. I have often felt that the future of Nudism is very much dependent upon its frank acknowledgment."

Welby's final paragraph sets out a hope that will be familiar to many naturists today:

> The future of Nudism, then, depends largely upon Nudists themselves. The leaders have it in their hands to build upon rock rather than sand, and if the existing fraternity and co-operation can be broadened, Nudism can hope for a prosperous future. Once the general public learn of the improved health and mental outlook which comes from Nudism, it may become almost universal.

This reprint of William Welby's *The Naked Truth About Nudism* is a valuable addition to the historiography of nudism and naturism, and I hope that you will enjoy reading Welby's thoughts and experiences, many of which remain relevant today.

Brian Curragh, MA
Archivist, British Naturism

Author's Preface

SINCE THE *Naked Truth About Nudism* was first published in 1935, the Nudist Movement has progressed considerably. Some of the Clubs described in "Clubs We Have Visited" have developed into much more important concerns, and general interest in the subject of Nudism has widened amazingly. So, at the request of the Publishers, I have undertaken to revise the original text and, to some extent, condense it in order that it may be published uniformly with my other books (*Naked and Unashamed* and *It's Only Natural*) in a 3/6 edition. I have taken great care in making necessary excisions to omit nothing which is really essential to a proper understanding of Nudism as it is practised to-day, and the additions are authoritative and mainly from first-hand knowledge. Of course, it is not possible, within the space at my command, to include all the changes and expansions which have taken place. They would fill a volume three times the dimensions of this one, but I do think I have included most of the really vital points which indicate the growth (and the direction of the growth) of the movement.

Nudism is now definitely "on the map." It is referred to in the Press, on the Radio, and is frequently encountered in popular cross-word puzzles. Most people know something of the movement, albeit their knowledge is sometimes limited and their ideas are somewhat distorted. Amongst those insufficiently informed there are still many misunderstandings to be cleared up, and there are points which have not been considered with sufficient thoroughness to enable Nudists themselves to realise their full significance. It is the aim of this book to enlighten the former and to prove helpful to the latter. The association of mixed sexes unclothed seems to be the real bugbear of the uninitiated, and this misunderstanding can only be dispelled, finally and completely, by actual experience. I feel confident, however, that after reading this book the most sceptical will realise that the sane practice of ventilating the skin and allowing it to absorb the life-giving rays of the sun will improve the health and add to the general enjoyment of life by all those adopting it.

William Welby
Essex, June, 1939.

CHAPTER I

What is Nudism?

WHAT IS NUDISM? Although Nudism has received a good deal of publicity, it is as difficult to define as Socialism and similar "isms." For the same reason, while the general basic principles are agreed, individuals differ considerably as to details. The "Back-to-Nature"Nudists (the "whole-hoggers," as one might say) eschew meat-eating, alcohol and tobacco. Again, some Nudists are enthusiastic in shedding their clothes in the open air, but dislike the idea of being without clothes indoors. Others, admitted extremists, like to spend all their leisure-time at home in the nude. Yet with all these differences there is a link—a sort of Freemasonry—between all Nudists and an earnest desire to be healthy and happy in a natural way.

Another thing which many people do not seem to appreciate is that Nudism is not just an ultra-modern cult. In Scandinavia, in Finland, even in Ireland, the practice of discarding clothes on certain occasions has been known for many generations. We do not need to go back to the times of the ancient Greeks, when the youth of both sexes competed publicly in athletic games and exercises in complete nudity, to realise that quite respectable people have seen no harm, and taken no harm, in the revealing of unclothed bodies. To children there is nothing disagreeable or disgusting in the sight of their own bodies, or those of others—until they have been taught that there is something—they are not told what—wrong or disgraceful in seeing, or being seen, without clothes. It is then that the seeds of curiosity are sown and the sexual parts endowed with an atmosphere of mystery and excitement which may later lead to undesirable consequences. It would hardly be too much to say that the majority of sexual faults and aberrations are largely due to this unwholesome and artificial atmosphere.

The more modern phase of Nudism, however, is founded upon sane and healthy principles and the outlook of Nudists generally is one of logic and commonsense. It may be said to have originated as an organised movement in Germany as a direct consequence of the War. No other country engaged in the World War of 1914-18 suffered quite so severely as Germany in the lowering of national physique. The people of Germany realised this, and took practical steps to overcome their handicap. Almost immediately the War was over, the "Wander Vogel," or bands of hikers, came into being. The youth of both sexes was inspired and encouraged to tramp about the country in free and easy costumes, camping in huts or in the open, with a freedom and enthusiasm that set an example to the World. Fresh air, exercise, and a spirit of camaraderie became almost a religion amongst the young people, and this earnest desire for healthy freedom was quite logically followed by the establishment of "Nacktkultur," or what we call Nudism. The Germans are a scientific nation. The value of sun and air was fully appreciated by them, and the utilisation of these gifts of Nature became another craze. The "Freikorperkultur," "Freilicht" and similar associations soon grew to a membership of between three and four millions, and these were not restricted to youth alone. Men and women of all ages and all classes joined in the movement, and a great many "foreigners" were attracted by the facilities for sun- and air-bathing and exercise "in the nude" offered in Germany which, at that time, were not available in their own countries. Some of these "foreigners" enjoyed themselves so much, and derived so much practical benefit from their visits, that they infected their friends with their own enthusiasm, and so groups began to form in other countries.

Under the Hitler regime, many of these camps and clubs have been closed down—not on account of their members being nude, but for political reasons. "Nacktkultur"was a progressive movement fostered by the Socialist Government and the Socialist municipalities and, as such, naturally came under restriction by the new Government, which no doubt regarded such communities as hot-beds for Socialistic activities. There were Public Sunbathing Parks, owned by municipalities somewhat on the lines of our own "Lansbury Lido" in Hyde Park, and the public swimming baths in Berlin were reserved two or three days a week for nude bathing. These no longer enjoy the approval of the Government. Private clubs, free from any political taint, however, were not interfered with and the first "Freilichtpark" of all—that instituted by Paul Zimmerman at Klingberg—is still inviting visitors from various countries. The example of Germany was soon followed by other countries, and clubs and camps were established in Austria, Belgium, England, France, Greece, Holland, Italy, Sweden, Switzerland, and America.

In England the movement has grown steadily and sanely. Many conservative people have been drawn to it by appreciation of the opportunities it affords for healthy freedom. Not a few clergymen are enthusiastic Nudists, and at least one has been bold enough to profess his faith in public and in print.

I will not, here, go into the various reasons why people become Nudists, because I propose to give, in a later chapter, some actual examples which have come to my knowledge at first hand. But I will try, with the reservations mentioned at the beginning of this chapter, to explain what is generally understood as Nudism by those who actually practise it.

First and foremost it is a means to health. The skin of the human body needs light and air just as much as plants do and you have only to think of the results of shutting up your plants in dark cells without ventilation, to realise that for your skin to be covered up with layers of clothing every hour in every year is a practical comparison, to appreciate that this is not a good thing for it. Fortunately, the human system is so extraordinarily adaptable that, after many generations, we who are accustomed to keep our bodies covered up have become almost immune to the evil consequences. The lamentable effects upon races unused to clothing when they have first been persuaded to it, however, are still within current memory. Natives of Polynesia, Micronesia and Melanesia, generally referred to as the South Sea Islands, have been decimated and some races have become almost extinct owing to the introduction of civilisation's first gifts—clothes and alcohol.

Loose clothing, and as little of it as possible, has long been recommended by medical men, and this certainly allows a greater amount of air to act upon the skin; but it is not as effectual as being without clothing altogether. Nor does it admit the beneficial effects of the light rays. To go back to our previous analogy, it is rather like keeping our plants in a cage of perforated zinc, which admits a certain amount of air but keeps out the light of the sun. Readers who are interested in gardening will be familiar with "earthing up" or brown-paper wrappers for "blanching" celery and other plants, and the effects upon a plant which, accidentally, has been covered up by an old box or piece of sacking. Without the action of light it is impossible for the plant to secrete the substance known as chlorophyll, which makes all vegetable life green. And this substance is essential to life. It is even sold in synthetic form as a remedy for lack of vitality and ill-health under a branded name, and is advertised extensively as the brand of chlorophyll. The occasional exposure of the skin to sun and air is therefore extremely beneficial to health and is one of the merits of Nudism. The one form of pride in which any Nudist, irrespective of physical beauty, can indulge is the clear, healthy-looking skin with a becoming tan which is gained by exposure to sun and wind. In addition, in a Nudist group of mixed sexes, there is a strong incentive to physical exercises to improve both health and appearance, which does not exist to the same extent under other conditions.

But while health is, in my opinion, the main plank in the platform of Nudism, it is not the only thing to be considered. The Director of a well-known Nudist Club, who said he "had nothing but praise" for *Naked and Unashamed*, suggested that I had stressed the physical side of Nudism, but had not fully emphasised the psychological value of the movement. The casting off of clothes does undoubtedly induce a feeling of freedom in the mind, as it does in the body. Anyone who has come home and changed from a business suit into a tennis shirt and flannels will have some idea of this feeling, but to be in the open air on a fine, sunny day, with no clothes on at all, accentuates it to the Nth degree. And the friendliness, frankness and general camaraderie of a Nudist group has never been equalled by any ordinary club. The practice of Nudism is, in itself, an indication of breadth of mind, a freedom from artificial and even petty conventions and affectations, to which most of us in everyday life conform without any logical thought. The community of interests in a Nudist camp exercises a remarkable social influence, and at the same time there is a chastening effect which develops feelings of refinement and good taste.

I am sorry that the question of sex seems to have formed so large a part in discussions on Nudism. So far from being an obsession, as some inexperienced people think, sex is far less emphasised in a Nudist community than it is at a dance or similar social function. Particularly on the feminine side. The alluring frocks which conceal and reveal at the same time; the various aids to sex appeal to which Modern Woman has access; sensuous music; rich foods and alcohol in tempting variety and the usually overheated atmosphere, are all lacking in a Nudist camp. There are no "sitting-out" places where flirtations and "petting" may be carried on, and it is certain that any member overstepping the line of true modesty would be instantly requested to resign. As I shall deal at greater length with the subordination of sex in Chapter IV, I need not dwell upon it here, but I hope to show, very clearly, that a very short time in a Nudist camp will blow away the cobwebs of sexual complexes far more effectively than any psycho-analysis or indoor debates upon the subject.

Right: *Countryside Charm.*

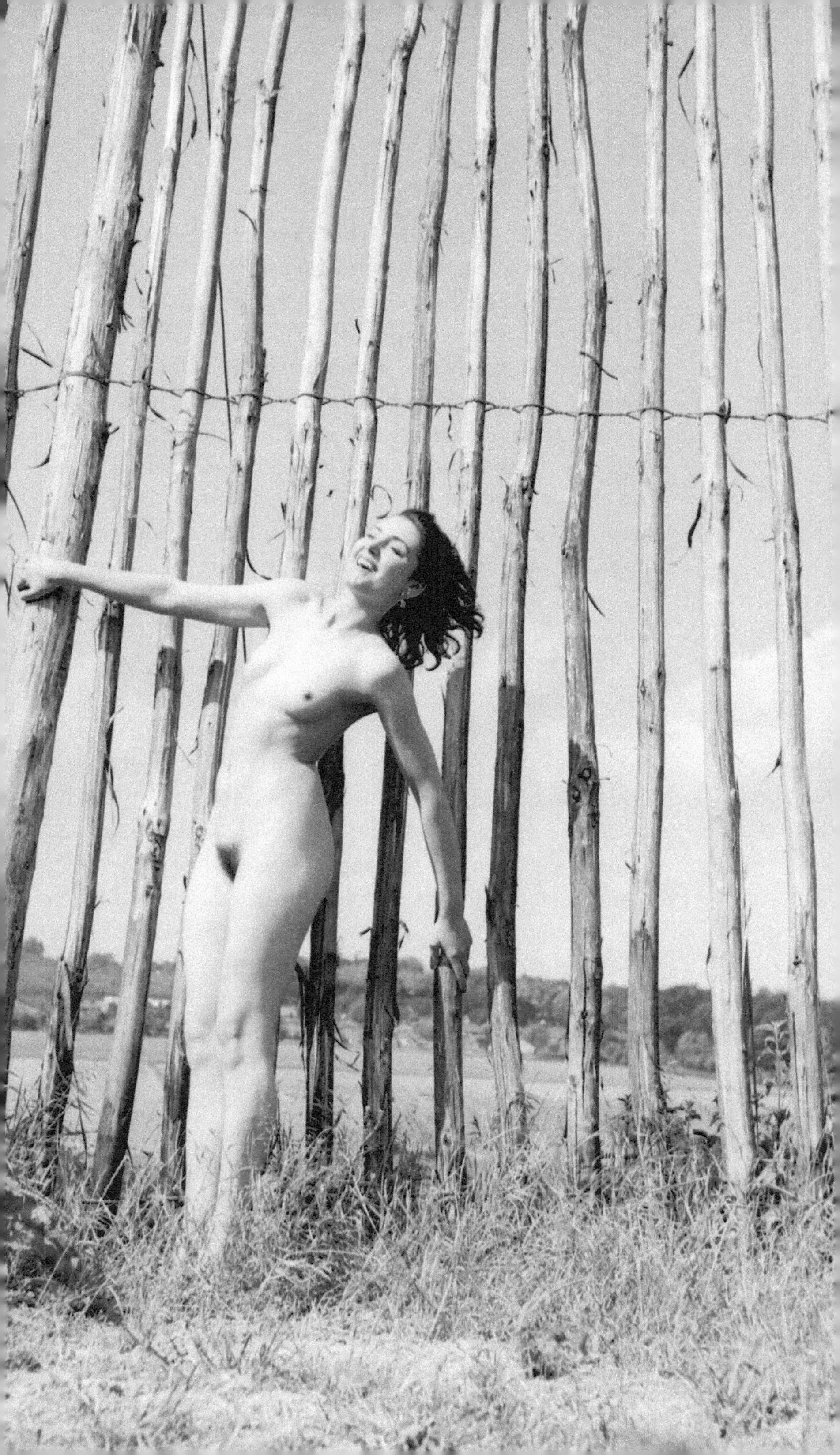

The question of diet, too, is not an essential of Nudist philosophy. The simple, almost primitive life in a Nudist camp tends to make people satisfied with simple foods, and there are a great many vegetarians in the Nudist ranks; but there is no dogmatic rule by which members must be bound. Alcohol is, quite wisely, I think, prohibited in Nudist camps and clubs, but Nudists are not all teetotallers. What they eat and drink when away from the community is entirely their own concern. Personally, I have not found any club where tobacco is prohibited, although I do know of Nudist enthusiasts who regard smoking as a form of self-poisoning entirely out of keeping with a movement mainly directed towards improvement in, and maintenance of, health.

I hope that by now the reader has begun to realise that Nudist groups are not composed of immoralists and faddists. That they do not pursue their activities without reason, and that even though the movement may not appeal to all, there is much to be said in its favour and no sound reason at all for condemning it. Those stupid individuals who have on occasion been prosecuted for appearing nude in public receive no more sympathy from real Nudists than they are likely to get from the world in general, and anyone who associates these eccentrics with the movement is sadly lacking in discrimination. Nudism is not a religious movement; it embraces members of all denominations including clergymen of the Church of England and Nonconformist Ministers. It is not a class movement; among its adherents will be found naval and military officers, doctors, members of the Bar, middle-class business men and women, clerks and typists. It has no political significance in this country, whatever associations it may have had in Germany or other countries. Its practitioners have no desire to proselytise, or carry out a crusade of conversion. Nudism is for you if, after careful study and consideration, it appeals to you. If it does not, there is no more to be said. It may be that some of your friends are Nudists without your knowing it or you may have friends of whose sensibility and respectability you are assured, who frankly and without hesitation will affirm their belief in, and sympathy for, the movement.

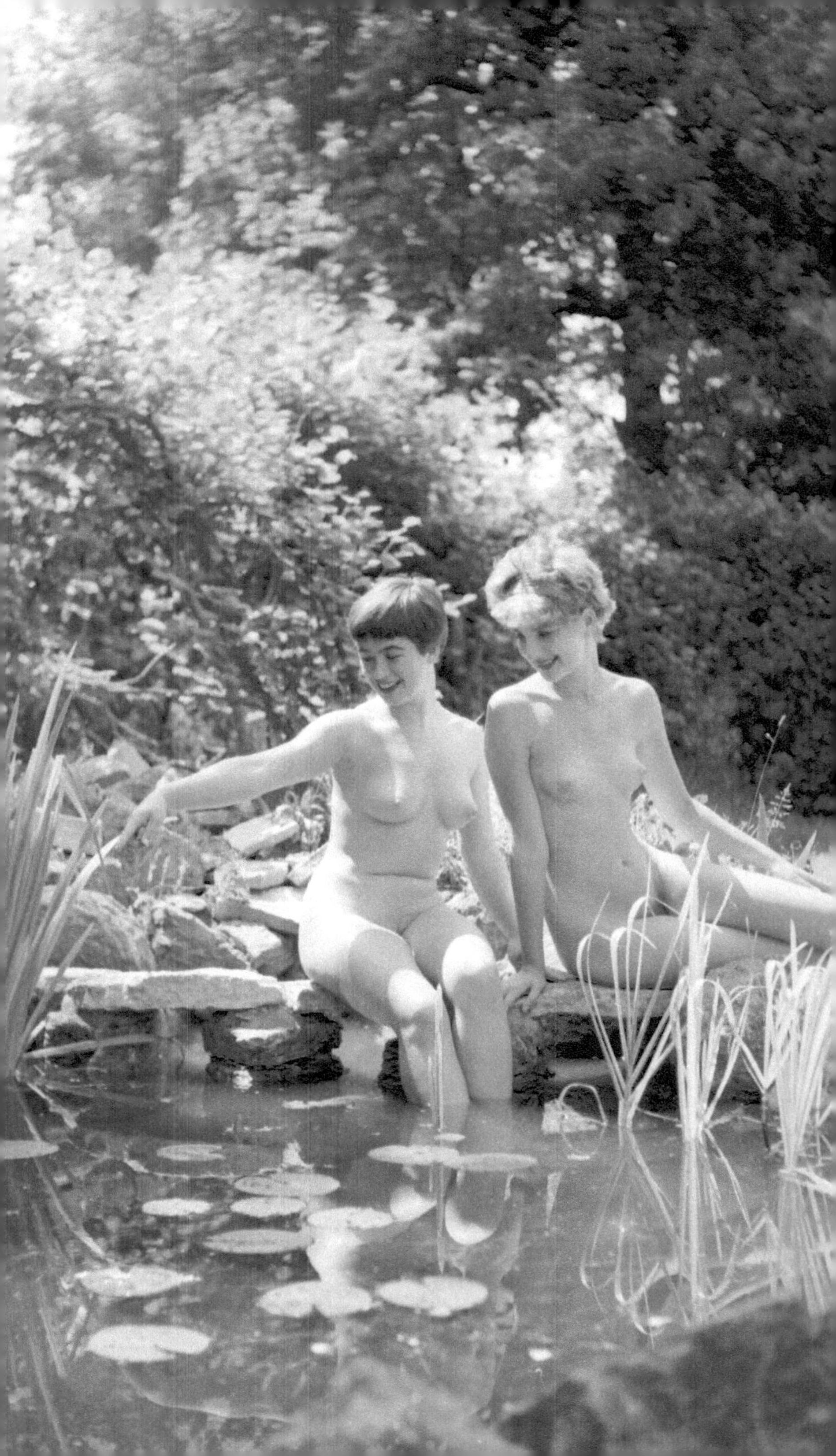

CHAPTER II

Nudism and Health

THIS IS NOT a medical book. Nor is it one of those pseudo medical books which, after an elaborate description of symptoms and treatment, finish up with "Call in the Doctor." But in dealing with the effects of Nudism on health, it will be necessary to clip into the lexicon of the medical man occasionally and to touch lightly on physiology and therapeutics. There is no doubt whatever that Nudism is an aid to health, and I shall endeavour to show how and why.

It is only comparatively recently that the importance of the skin has been properly appreciated. Cleanliness and friction have, of course, for centuries been understood as beneficial to health. In the days of the Greeks and Romans, baths and massage were almost a matter of routine. It may not be common knowledge that what we call "Turkish" baths are really "Roman" baths—introduced to the Turks by their Roman conquerors. During the Roman occupation of Britain these baths were quite common here; but, like many excellent Roman institutions, they disappeared after the invasions of the barbaric Danes and Saxons and were not re-adopted for some centuries. The exudation of poisons through the skin by perspiration is a very ancient remedy and is still employed in the modern practice of Medicine. This is what is really

---

Left: *By Rock and Pool.*

meant by the expression "A good, healthy sweat." To prevent clogging of the pores, frequent bathing, with a good rub-down, is necessary, and this enables the skin not only to throw off poisonous exudations, but also to absorb health-giving qualities from the air. Our skin needs air as much as our lungs. Modern science has discovered that the skin has even more important functions to perform. We know now that the skin must be regarded as an organ similar to the stomach, kidneys and liver. In other words, it is a sort of chemical factory, that absorbs raw materials and turns them into something else. It effects chemical changes. It is assisted in those changes particularly by the action of light. The absorption of light by the skin, apart from being a necessity of health, has been proved actually to cure some forms of disease. That exposure of the skin to direct sunlight produced curative results is not a new idea. It was known to, and taken advantage of, by the Ancients. The composition of the spectrum and the effects of various rays, however, is a relatively modern discovery, and even now much research work is being undertaken which may lead to still further enlightenment. In addition to the visible rays of the spectrum, such as we see in a rainbow, it was discovered that at either end of the spectrum were *invisible* rays—at one end the ultraviolet, and at the other end the infra-red. These rays have been proved to have almost miraculous properties. Used conjunctively they act as a remarkable tonic. The ultraviolet are cold rays and the infra-red are heat rays. The ultraviolet rays penetrate but a very short way below the surface of the skin and are completely blocked out by any form of clothing. The infra-red are deeply penetrating rays and reach right into the tissues of the body. In order to bring the bloodstream near the surface of the skin, within reach of the ultraviolet rays, heat is necessary, and therefore to get the full tonic effects of light treatment the infra-red rays must be included. For the moment, however, we are only concerned with the *effects* of the rays and not the means of inducing them. The sun being the source of all light, it is obvious that all rays are included in natural sunlight. Given free access, sunlight will enable the skin to store up the important "Vitamin D," and if a sufficient quantity is accumulated during the summer months, our system is enabled to draw upon this supply during the winter months, just as a thrifty person is able to draw upon savings in times of adversity.

Amongst the various factors upon which vitality depends are the activities of the "endocrine" glands. Ordinary glands have ducts through which the substances they secrete may flow to other parts of the system; but endocrine glands are those which have no ducts and have no means of passing on their secretions except through the bloodstream itself. They are therefore called "ductless" glands and they elaborate substances known as "hormones," which are essential to our well-being. These hormones are carried by the bloodstream to all parts of the body and affect the functional activity of distant organs. The endocrine glands are particularly responsive to light treatment, so that the beneficial effects of sunlight (real or artificial) depend largely upon the rays reaching them. Amongst the most important of these glands are the thyroid, pituitary, and those concerned with sexual functions.

Keeping in view these simple physiological facts, it is not difficult to see several ways in which Nudism can be an aid to health. If the whole of the skin is exposed to the air it will be encouraged to greater activity. Just as the inhaling of fresh air, or oxygen, through the lungs purifies the blood and stimulates the action of the heart, so does light and air invigorate the skin and help it to carry out its functions more rapidly and more efficiently. Poisonous vapours are exhaled freely and fresh vitalising elements are absorbed. The skin is really a kind of "thermostat"—that is, an automatic controller of temperature such as is used on incubators, motor-cars, and in large modern buildings. It is intended by Nature to control the temperature of our bodies, but, unfortunately, through being coddled and hampered by clothing it has, in most of us, lost a great deal of its power. The average person, who is unused to going without clothes, is very sensitive to the temperature of the surrounding air when unaccustomed parts of the body are exposed. This is not, as many people think, natural. It simply means that the skin is not doing its job. Any muscle or limb which, through illness or accident, is out of use for some time becomes weak and inefficient. After a long time in bed we find that we have "lost the use of our legs." But nobody would be so absurd as to suggest that we ought always to walk about with the aid of crutches. Yet that is really a parallel to our feeling chilly when certain parts of our body are uncovered. I have often worked and played in my garden through a hot summer day wearing nothing but a pair of cotton "rugger-shorts" and sandals, and later in the evening, when the temperature has been many degrees lower, I have sat on the verandah, talking or listening to the radio, without making any change in my attire. My skin has been as cold to the touch as a piece of wet marble, and yet, inwardly, I have felt "as warm as toast." Of course, this acclimatisation must be acquired gradually. To sit outdoors on a cold day with little or no clothing, as an experiment, would be extremely foolish and even dangerous. On the other hand, on the Continent and in America, ski-ing and skating parties wearing nothing but boots and socks are by no means uncommon. Some of my own acquaintances have worked on camp clearing here in England in mid-winter in the same garb. There is the very old story of a high official from England watching tobogganing and snow sports in Canada. He was well wrapped up in furs, but felt the intense cold keenly. Near him was an Indian chief clad in nothing but breech-clout, leggings and moccasins. The British personage expressed astonishment that the chief did not feel terribly cold, and the Indian pointed to his face. "You feel cold there?" he asked. "No!" said his Lordship "but that is my face." "Well!" replied the Indian, rubbing his hand over his chest and stomach, "Me all face."

Probably few, if any, would deny the desirability of cleansing the body, at least occasionally, by means of a bath, hot or cold yet to be satisfied with exposing the face and hands to air and light is equivalent to claiming that the washing of hands and face is all that is necessary. Then there are various glands to be considered. Deprived of light they cannot function with complete efficiency. Many eminent medical men are enthusiastic supporters of actino-therapy, or the treatment of disease by light, and some wonderful results have been achieved in this way. It has been proved that, apart from the tonic properties of light, the sun has a definite bactericidal power. Few germs can survive a substantial dose of sunlight. Malignant growths can be arrested, and in some cases destroyed, by light treatment. The secretion of hormones can be increased and a general toning-up of the system achieved by this means. Now, if it has already been proved, and it has, that disease can be cured by submitting affected parts to the action of light, is it unreasonable to infer that exposure of the whole body must be beneficial? And if it is good to combat disease in this way, is it not even better to *prevent* ill-health by similar means? I do not wish it to be thought that I am recommending Nudism as a "cure-all." I believe, from personal experience and reliable evidence, that its practice is a definite aid to health; but I am by no means a fanatic. Nor do I think everyone a suitable subject. Constitutionally or psychologically, the practice of Nudism may be quite unsuitable to many people. We all know the value of physical culture by means of scientifically-planned exercises, but they are not always suitable for people of delicate or feeble constitutions. There are cases where "one man's meat is another man's poison." Harm can be done, too, by over-exposure to direct sunlight. Those who may be prevented from dangerous exposure in cold weather by a feeling of chilliness and dis-comfort may, under the genial influence of the sun, unwisely protract their exposure until they have done themselves more harm than good. Erythema, or reddening of the skin, does not usually appear until some hours after the ultra-violet rays have acted upon the skin, and if the skin has been badly burned, it is then too late to do anything but apply palliatives in the form of unguents.

Actual "sun-burn" should be avoided, but if moderate exposures, increased by easy stages, are adopted, the skin will gradually "tan" and provide its own protection. "Tanning" is really "pigmentation," the forming of pigment in the skin, which is Nature's method of filtering the ultra-violet rays and preventing any excess reaching the more delicate tissues. It follows that parts of the body usually unexposed will naturally be more sensitive to the rays and must be treated with even greater care than hands and face and arms. The use of oils and lotions is of but small value after damage has been done, but, as a preventive, cocoanut oil well rubbed into the skin before exposure is decidedly useful. This is preferable to olive oil and at the same time less expensive; the slight odour, which may be disliked by some people, soon evaporates in the open air. It is quite a mistake to regard lying in the sun for protracted periods as a health-giving sun-bath. This is far more likely to cause enervation, irritability and dizziness. It is delightful to bask in the comforting rays of the sun and relax occasionally, but some form of exercise is essential. In Nudist camps there is always work to be done for those who feel inclined to it, and it may vary in strenuousness from felling trees to gathering sticks for the fire. There is great variety in the games and sports which may be enjoyed in the freedom from clothes—Tennis, Badminton, Tenniquoit, Volley-ball and Archery, amongst others, varying with the resources of the Club. Where swimming pools are available they are sure to prove popular.

Another way in which Nudism is an aid to health is the encouragement it offers to physical culture. One needs to be of stern moral fibre conscientiously to carry out regular exercises in the solitude of the bedroom or bathroom; but with the moral support of fellow members imbued with a spirit of enthusiasm and friendly rivalry and the example of trained athletes of both sexes, there is real enjoyment to be derived from health-giving and beautifying exercises. Solitary exercises are very much like diaries; many people start them, but few keep them up permanently. We are all, consciously or unconsciously, influenced by vanity, and where no clothes are worn there is a strong incentive to improve the appearance of the body. Nudist communities offer incentive, example and opportunity for the improvement of physique in a greater degree than any other social organisation known to me. The fact that the whole of the body is visible to other members of both sexes is a cogent reason for taking a practical personal interest in physical culture. Exercises under these conditions make a much stronger appeal to children than those taken under compulsion at school, and the middle-aged, even those past middle age, are induced to take part in activities which would not be considered in other circumstances. I have noticed a remarkably youthful spirit amongst comparatively elderly persons of both sexes when taking part in these games and exercises, and I have myself found the freedom and invigorating effects of being without clothes an inducement to greater physical activity. Health also depends a great deal on psychology, and the mental freedom which accompanies bodily freedom is an important factor. Various complexes exist in our subconscious selves, in greater or lesser degree, which may in some cases lead to neuroses, the causes of which are unsuspected. Inhibitions and repressions, founded upon a sense of shame or fear, are often attributable to misunderstandings associated with sex, and may be relieved or dissipated, without recourse to a psycho-analyst, by the simple and harmless recreation of a Nudist group. When whole families play and work together in a state of nudity the mind is free from any sense of shame or excitement with regard to those parts of the body connected wlth sexual functions. This freedom, especially in the case of children, saves much tension of the nerves which may otherwise be artificially built up. Once it is realised that no part of the body is in itself shameful or disgusting, the sexual parts cease to have any special significance and attract no more attention or thought than a hand or foot. An authority on sex, Dr. F. B. Rocstro, writing of the effects of Nudism on sexual potency, says: "My personal experience has been that sexual intercourse is sought less frequently, but that the relief obtained has been greater and more satisfying both mentally and physically."

I have expressed regret that the question of sex should be given such prominence in discussions on Nudism, and I do feel that this aspect has, in many instances, been unduly emphasised, but sex and health are so closely associated that it is not desirable that the association should be altogether ignored. Individuals in whom sex forms an obsession are not suitable subjects for Nudism, and their self-consciousness would probably prove a bar to their ever feeling at home in a Nudist group. Indeed, it is extremely doubtful if they would even get so far as applying for membership. To normal persons, with a simple and natural interest in sex, such associations may be beneficial, inasmuch as they will tend to prevent the formation of sex-complexes.

To a real Nudist, sex is quite a subordinate matter and the encouragement to spend more time in the open air, to become healthily tired by physical exercise of one kind or another, to enjoy light and simple meals in congenial company amid natural surroundings, will be found an antidote to hypersthesia and undue estimation of sex.

Physically, by acting as a tonic to the whole system and by building up increased resistance to disease and minor complaints, exposure of the whole body to sun and air will improve the health generally, and psychologically it will improve the mind and nerves by the freedom and social interest which is one of the essential features of a Nudist community. And since the social effects are of considerable importance, let us consider them in the next Chapter, "Social Nudism."

CHAPTER III

Social Nudism

MAN IS BY nature a gregarious animal and derives more pleasure from acting in concert with his fellows than from solitary pursuits. This is the foundation of all sorts of clubs and associations from the local tennis or bowling club to the world-wide organisation of Freemasonry and similar societies. It is indeed natural and desirable that Man should keep in close contact with Mankind to develop and consolidate the best of his characteristics; solitude induces selfishness, morbidity and sluggishness of mind. We shall find, on consideration, that the advantages of social intercourse apply to Nudism as they do to other phases of human life. I have known people admit, in a rather condescending way, that the exposure of the body to sun and air may be beneficial to health; but why, they ask, must one join a club and mix with a crowd of both sexes to enjoy these benefits? The answer is very simple in one sense, but very complicated in another.

From the purely physical point of view (no thinking creature *can* be considered from the purely physical point of view, actually) there are certain handicaps. Very few are so fortunately situated that they can expose themselves in the open air without risk of being seen by others who, not being Nudists, would be shocked by the sight; and the danger of prosecution for "indecent exposure" is by no means negligible. Possibly on rare occasions a secluded cove by the sea may tempt to a bathe without a costume and perhaps a limited sun-bath after; but, as things are at present, a certain amount of fear must accompany such an adventure and no regularity can be counted upon. In the average private garden the difficulty of securing complete exposure while being safely obscured from other eyes is so great that only a fanatic would attempt to overcome it.

Where, then, can the average person expose his body to the life-giving rays of the sun and caressing currents of air without risking offence to others and interference with himself? I can think of only two situations where this would be possible—in some far-off country where nudity provokes no comment, or in a Nudist club at home. Here, if he wishes, he can sun-bathe in perfect security without taking part in any of the social activities of the club and without being regarded as a dangerous eccentric. It is true that he may see other nude people, of both sexes, in his comings and goings, but he can ignore them, as they will ignore him, when he desires privacy. Delicacy of feeling and absence of intrusion are rather more pronounced in a Nudist club than elsewhere. I do not, however, believe that any normal person would seek isolation once he came in contact with the sympathetic atmosphere of a Nudist camp. Friendliness, the desire to be mutually helpful, and a community of interests, will be found more marked here than in almost any other gathering.

Freedom from self-consciousness makes Nudists readier to form acquaintanceship and more sincere in conversation. Generally speaking, too, their intelligence is higher than the average. They are given to reading and travelling and, above all, thinking; most of them have had interesting experiences (quite apart from Nudism) which fit in with talks on all sorts of subjects and add both charm and ease to speaker and listener alike.

In an otherwise eulogistic review of my book, *Naked and Unashamed*, one reviewer disagreed with my saying that "it is impossible to stand on one's dignity or act snobbishly when bereft of the trappings of class or caste," and he claimed that class distinction and snobbishness can be found just as much in Nudist circles as in any other. It was not my intention to suggest that a well-bred and well-educated man or woman would be indistinguishable from one lacking these advantages. I prefaced the words quoted above by saying that "the feeling of intimacy which association in the nude must inevitably bring about would make for greater friendliness and give encouragement to the communal spirit." I have found this to be true of every gathering of Nudists at which I have been present.

Certainly there is a difference in the social standing between one club and another; the difference in fees and subscriptions accounts for this to a great extent, and as most clubs select their members very carefully, it is quite natural that they should maintain a standard suited to their membership. No one of intelligence would suggest that the conversation and companionship of an illiterate person are as enjoyable to cultured people as those of one of their own class. What I mean by "snobbishness" is the artificial attitude of the semi-cultured or plutocratic individual who has, in his own opinion, "raised himself above" his class and is afraid that other people will not realise it. One hardly ever finds the really well-bred "snobbish" in this sense.

Apart, therefore, from the amenities of a suitable site in, perhaps, a beautiful woodland with shelters, a swimming pool and other advantages unavailable to the solitary sun-bather, there is much to be said for the actual social life of a Nudist camp. First, there is the feeling of absolute freedom when you have "cast your clouts" and stepped forth "naked and unashamed." You experience a sensation of increased physical well-being, and when you join a group of fellow members you feel at ease generally. You do not feel that you are a peculiar person doing something eccentric, because all your companions are doing the same and enjoying it.

You can either join in a friendly and animated discussion, have a quiet chat with an acquaintance, or take part in one of the many games which are usually available. You will find a definite encouragement to physical exercise, either in games or carefully-planned exercises under a qualified instructor. It is quite different from the "daily dozen" in your bathroom or bedroom. Something of the competitive spirit is introduced without jealousy. You will be pleased to find you can perform better than "A," and you will want to try hard to equal "Z." When it is all over, you may seek light refreshment or, if the time is opportune, you may have lunch or tea on a grassy slope or reclining in a deck-chair with a group of merry companions.

You may have your own hut or tent and form your own family group, or you may join in a larger party.

In conversation there is freedom from conventional restraint without objectionable license. There is a spirit of practical helpfulness, too. If you need assistance in erecting a tent or hut, willing volunteers are at hand to give it. Usually the work of clearing and improving the sites is undertaken by members themselves, and this offers excellent opportunities for developing the communal spirit.

All the social advantages of any ordinary club are attained in a Nudist club, with the addition of this delightful freedom of body and spirit, and that is why Nudism may be considered as a social force.

Compare these conditions with those of the individual who, through foolish prejudices or lack of understanding, endeavours to take his sun-bath in solitary seclusion. It must be carried out clandestinely, and this in itself must imbue him with a vague sense of guilt—a feeling that he is doing something of which he might well be ashamed, since if his neighbours were to see him he would certainly be ostracised, even if he escaped legal prosecution. His solitude leads to introspection, and he may begin to wonder if indeed there is not some atavistic impulse behind it—some throw-back to distant primitive or savage ancestors. And if he persists after this feeling is once aroused, he is on the way to complexes and neuroses which will do him more harm than the ultra-violet and infra-red rays will do him good. If he attempts to perform physical exercises, it is more than likely that they will have so little spirit in them as to be valueless. He cannot play games without someone to play with. He will miss that vital spirit of camaraderie which is characteristic of every Nudist community. He may, perhaps, practise Nudism in his home, indoors, free from alien observation and criticism; but still the psychological effect is the same—unless he has Nudist friends who will join him and turn the affair from a solitary one into a social one. Then he will be gaining some of the advantages of a Nudist club and forsaking his idea of individualism.

One of the real advantages of social Nudism is that it completely disposes of a lot of nonsense which is thought and spoken about the unclothed figure of the opposite sex. There is a great difference between observing an isolated individual of the opposite sex unclothed and watching a large group of the two sexes all perfectly at ease and quite indifferent to the fact that they are nude.

In order that there may be no possible misunderstanding as to what I mean by "social Nudism," I should like to make it clear that I refer to the equivalent, apart from the lack of clothing, of such social gatherings as tennis clubs, dances, family reunions and similar meetings for mutual enjoyment.

Having practised both, I can say with confidence that there is no comparison between solitary sun-bathing and social Nudism. Strange as it may seem to the uninitiated, one is far less self-conscious in a community of Nudists than naked and alone. The fact that all one's companions are in the same state makes nudity seem quite insignificant, and the knowledge that their ideas on the subject are in harmony imparts a feeling of confidence and satisfaction unknown to the solitary. There is no boredom, such as may creep in when one has nothing to do and no one to talk to. There is an unquestionable broadening of the mind by the exchange of opinions and experiences, and since narrow-minded and ignorant persons are not likely to be found in a Nudist community, mental alertness is maintained at a high level.

Of course, Nudists are not all cast in one mould. Just as there are physical differences between individual members, some short and some tall, some fat and some thin (as in any other society), so there are psychological differences. Although

I have not met any fanatics so far, I have met vegetarians, teetotallers and non-smokers. I think in every case they have adopted these creeds purely as a question of health, and their attitude has been one of tolerance towards those who differ from them.

On one occasion I and my wife and a friend were confined, by a heavy rainstorm, to the tent of a lady whose husband was a "Nature doctor." After a time, my craving for a cigarette grew so strong that, with some misgiving, I asked if she would mind my smoking in her tent. She laughed and said if I was so silly as to want to poison myself with a narcotic it was entirely my own affair and would not affect her in the least.

I have one Nudist friend who feels the same regarding alcohol, but he has accompanied me in an hotel where we have chatted over drinks, mine alcoholic and his nonalcoholic.

It has been said that the true proof of tolerance is to be tolerant of the intolerant, and I think this will apply to practically all Nudist groups. They do not get angry because those who understand nothing of the movement condemn it. They simply pass over such criticism with good-humoured indifference. They agree that for some, for one reason or another, Nudism may be unsuitable; but for kindred spirits they have always a warm welcome and a sincere desire to make the novice entirely at home as quickly as possible. And, judging from personal observation and experience, they are remarkably apt at doing so.

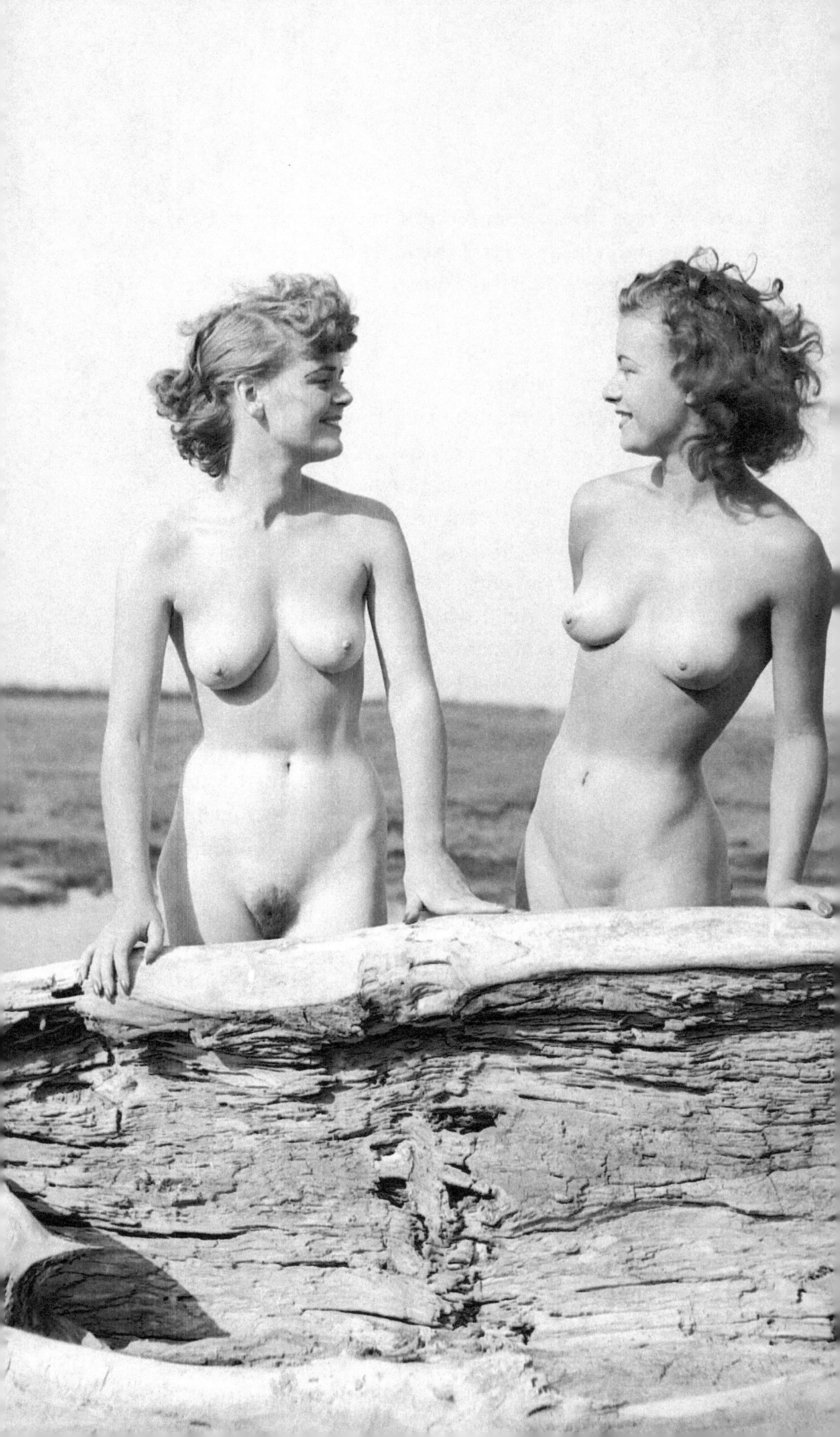

CHAPTER IV

Subordination of Sex

IT MAY SEEM a little inconsistent, after expressing my regret that "sex" has been so much emphasised in connection with Nudism, to devote a chapter of my book to this subject; but it is an aspect which has to be considered and one which is the least understood by ignorant critics of the movement.

The reader may notice that I have chosen the title *"Subordination* of Sex,"which is a very different thing from the *suppression* of sex. If I may indulge in a little further apparent paradox, I would say that what we suffer from to-day is a combination of too much suppression of sex and too much exaggeration of its importance. On the one hand we get a hypocritical pretence that no such thing exists, and on the other that it is the one vital factor of our existence. Both pretensions are equally absurd. No normal person is wholly insensitive to the influence of sex. Some of the highest attributes of human nature—unselfishness, tenderness, self-sacrifice, self-respect and ambition are all developed by it. I believe a healthily-sexed individual leads a fuller and more intelligent life than one under-sexed.

Sex often gives inspiration to artists, whether painters, writers or musicians. And it is an absolutely natural phenomenon; we should none of us be here at all were it not for the

---

Left: *Between Friends.*

almost miraculous powers of sex. Why, then, should children be brought up in ignorance or deception concerning the very cause of their existence and what may prove to be one of the most vital factors of their later life? Why should adolescents and adults regard it as a subject fit only for innuendo and secrecy? Far more harm is done by forcing thoughts and conversations on the subject into submerged channels than clean, healthy discussion in the open could do.

It may be that, to avoid dangerous consequences, the immature mind needs guidance and the unformed character support in responsibility, but ignorance lends no assistance to either, and the suggestion that sex is unclean or wicked is a distortion of facts which may lead to incalculable harm. On the other hand, undue insistence upon the importance of sex may lead to obsessions which are physically and psychologically disastrous. One of the most illogical and ridiculous of sex conventions is the idea that it is shameful and dangerous to expose certain parts of the human body. Anyone child, adolescent or adult—can observe the sexual organs of an animal without any sense of indecency. Even an old maid may have her pet cat or dog and remain unshocked by the exposure of the whole of its body. The truth is that there is nothing indecent in the sight of a naked man or woman, except the convention which gives rise to the idea. Those who have been brought up to regard the nude body in this way may be shocked or agreeably titillated at the sight, according to the condition or calibre of the mind. They may be affected in the same way by a picture or a statue. It may be taken as axiomatic, however, that complete nudity has actually a chastening effect in contrast with semi-nudity or provocative styles in dress.

In my young days it was regarded as rather a "thrill" to see a lady board an omnibus and expose her ankles and a few inches of lacy petticoat; but a few years ago, when knee-length skirts were common, no one took the slightest notice of about a yard of silk stocking containing a shapely leg. Convention decreed that such an exhibition was quite "decent" and so no one was offended and, in fact, no one was interested. It is the same in a Nudist gathering. Where everyone is nude, no one is conspicuous. Curiosity is disarmed, and with it pruriency and impure thoughts.

If association in the nude excited sexual feelings, it would, for obvious reasons, be impossible for a single Nudist club to remain in existence. If it destroyed the natural impulses of sexual sympathy and rendered those who practise it sexless, it would not appeal to the thousands of husbands and wives who are enthusiastic Nudists to-day.

There is, in all normal persons, a perfectly natural desire for the company of the opposite sex, apart from love or lust. The sexes are complementary to each other, and many delightful friendships can be formed on a basis of comradeship and community of interests. This is the sort of thing which is fostered in a Nudist club. The inevitable slight difference in point of view adds interest and liveliness to a discussion between opposite sexes, and each can gain something from the conversation of the other. With all ideas of sex relegated to the background, instead of being aroused by frocks and frills designed directly or indirectly to that end, such a happy consummation is more easily and more certainly attained.

Artificial stimulus to sexual thought is almost always caused by curiosity and anticipation. The semi-nudity displayed in some stage-shows or cabaret entertainments and in Continental bordels are deliberate attempts to arouse eroticism, and to the unsophisticated these devices do undoubtedly act as a stimulant; but complete nudity is a different thing altogether, and in suitable environment has not the least erotic effect.

It will be seen from what I have said that, so far from the intermixing of sexes in a state of nudity leading to licentiousness or the augmentation of sexual passions, it has exactly the reverse effect. I know it is difficult for some people to realise this, and probably nothing but practical, personal experience would convince these; but if they have any friends who are Nudists, a little reflection should enable them to judge whether such are of the type to whom undesirable sex associations are likely to appeal. Particularly if these friends have families, I would like them to observe the demeanour and conversation of the children. Children are an important factor in the consideration of this subject. We know with what success they have been brought up in apparent ignorance and seclusion. The late Dr. Mary Scharlieb, that grand old dame who carried on her practice till she died at a ripe old age, said when writing on this subject:— "It is certain that the conspiracy of silence which has lasted so many years has brought forth nothing but evil." In every school, whether of boys or girls, there will be school-fellows ready and eager to impart sex knowledge as they understand it. Verbal initiation will very likely be supplemented by obscene drawings of a very crude type and a somewhat distorted introduction to human anatomy. Children whose parents have taken them amongst Nudists will be immune to the ill effects of such instruction. Instead of having the thrill of a somewhat "naughty" adventure, it will seem merely silly and uninteresting. They will have more accurate knowledge than their teachers and familiarity with the sight of nakedness will make them indifferent to undesirable presentations of it. Young men and young women are apt at times to let their imaginations dwell upon sex, even though it may be more or less subconsciously, and here again the practice of Nudism is beneficial. Mere physical attributes partially revealed will cease to excite curiosity and a train of thought leading to eroticism, once the whole of the body has become familiar by sight. For these reasons Nudism does subordinate sex without in any sense repressing it, and by so doing is favourable to health, psychologically as well as physically.

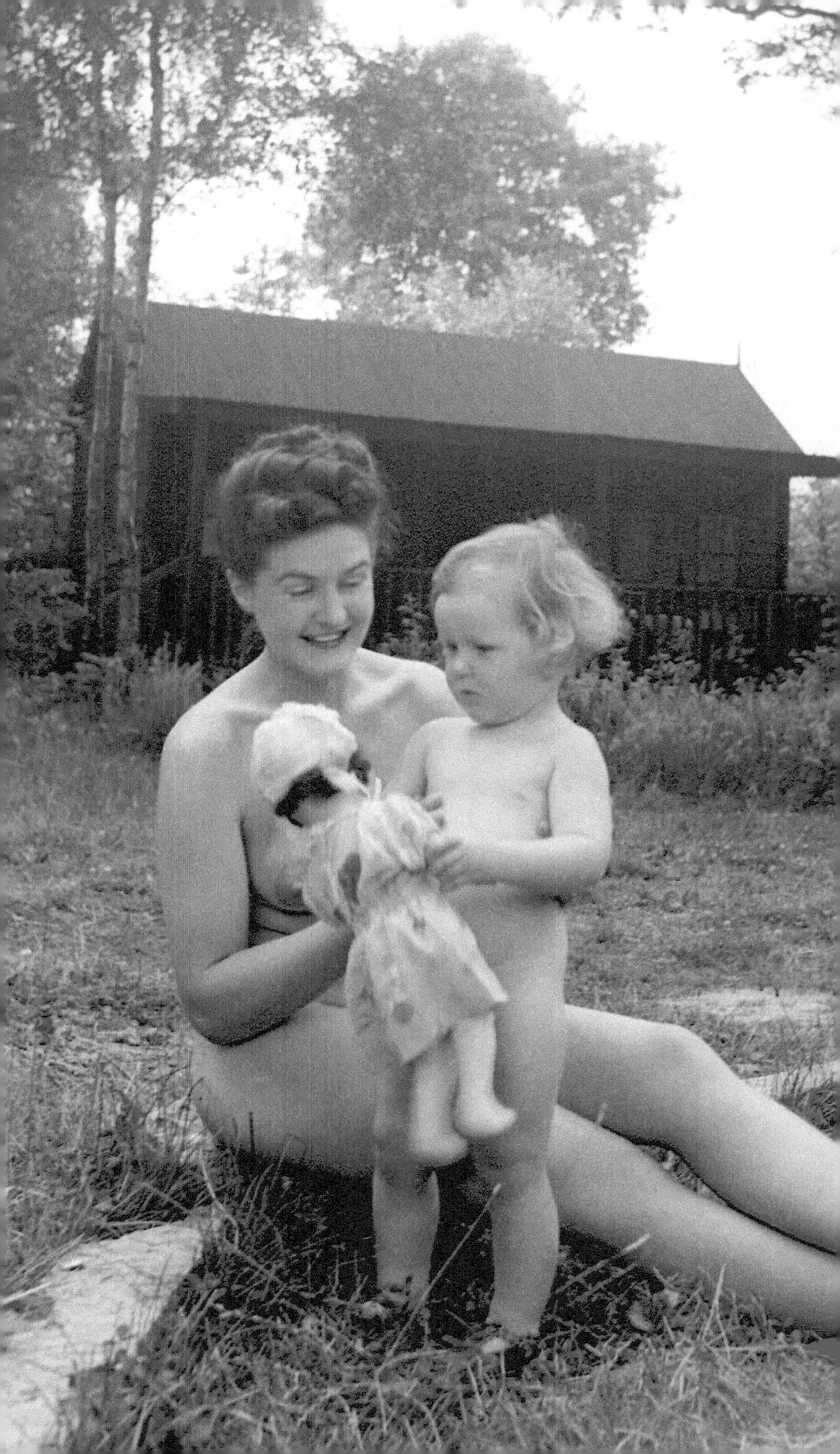

CHAPTER V

Why They Become Nudists

A GREAT MANY of the uninitiated must wonder how and why people become Nudists. Some of my friends have asked me "what sort of people" one meets in a Nudist club or what "Nudists are like." My reply has been that Nudists are exactly like the people one meets in an omnibus or on an Underground train or in the street. In other words, they include all types, and there is nothing to distinguish them from non-Nudists. As I said in the last chapter, they are usually more given to thinking and reasoning than the average individual, but there is nothing in their appearance or manner to stamp them as Nudists. As to how and why they join the movement, that will best be explained by quoting a few examples personally known to me. The great majority have been attracted in the first place by reasons of health. As I know more about my own case than I know of any other, and more than any other can know of it, I will tell you first about myself.

As a boy I was always fond of the open air and freedom in the way of clothing. During one year of my boyhood I spent the greater part of my time with the local fishermen, helping them with their boats and gear, and being rewarded with sailing

---

Left: *Shared Moments.*

trips and odd scraps of information which I hoped would one day prove useful to me. Like so many boys of that period, my ambition was to become an apprentice in the Mercantile Marine. My parents did not share this ambition. For one thing, I was told, I was much too delicate and could never stand the hardships. I am afraid I was rather an argumentative child, and I certainly was inquisitive. I decided to put the question of my hardiness to the test. On most of my trips I wore a cricket shirt (well open at the neck), a pair of old flannel trousers, socks and sand-shoes. This was my garb, summer and winter, when I could manage it without getting into trouble. At night I generally slept nude, covered with a single blanket. Once, as a test, I waited until everyone was fast asleep and then climbed out of my bedroom window and down a rainwater pipe, and spent the night on the sands returning in time to be found in bed when the rest of the household awakened. I also became interested in gymnastics and physical exercises, and used dumbbells and, later on, a "Sandow Developer." Unfortunately, when I came to London and started life in an office, I gradually lost my interest in physical health, although I was still fond of walking and cycling and bathing. Many years before ultraviolet rays were talked of, I used to tell my bathing companions that I enjoyed rolling about nude on the sunny sands more than the bathe itself, and felt it did me more good. In my new life I began to deteriorate physically for some years until I went to Canada and worked on a farm. This revived my interest in health and strength, and I came home very fit. For the next twenty years I settled down once more to an indoor sedentary life except during the War, when I travelled all over the country on Government service and finished up rather a wreck owing to irregular feeding and insufficient sleep. A few years ago I had a bad bout of influenza which led to a nervous breakdown, from which I did not recover for some months. At the time I did not much care whether I got better or not (a symptom of the complaint, no doubt), but when I did get better, I determined to avoid a similar experience at all costs. A Harley Street specialist said that I suffered from a deficiency of vitamin "D" and calcium, and prescribed a certain branded food containing vitamin "D" and haemoglobin, amongst other things, and tablets composed of calcium lactate and sodium lactate. Deficiencies in vitamin "D" and calcium usually go together, as the system will not absorb calcium when vitamin "D" is lacking. I began to study my health from this point of view, and realising that vitamin "D" is a "sunshine" vitamin I determined to get as much sunshine as possible. I spent a great deal of time in my garden, and, starting with a tennis shirt and flannel trousers, gradually exposed more and more of my skin to the sun and air. A short-sleeved sports shirt and flannel shorts led eventually to my wearing nothing but a pair of cotton gym. shorts and sandals. My health improved so much that it became a topic of conversation amongst my friends. When winter came I was handicapped, but I bought myself a "sun-ray" lamp and continued the treatment. This was not equal to the summer exposure in the open air, but it is significant that I, who had suffered badly hitherto, was the only one of the family to be absolutely free from colds for two winters in succession.

The practical benefit I had derived from exposure induced me to investigate the merits of Nudism, and I studied the subject very closely from all angles. I read practically everything that was printed about the subject, and supplemented my reading with personal enquiries wherever and whenever possible. I thought it all out, and then wrote my book, *Naked and Unashamed*. I was not a Nudist then, but the remarkable success of the book brought me invitations to visit various Nudist clubs, and after my first real experience (described in the "Author's Preface" to the second and subsequent editions), I became an enthusiastic Nudist myself. My wife was quite agreeable to the idea in the abstract, but became almost "panicky" when we were on our way to our initiation. We have to thank Mr. J. W. Joseph, the Secretary of the New Forest Club, and his charming wife for our happy introduction. We thoroughly enjoyed our visit, and found, in practice, all the delights and advantages we had considered in theory only hitherto. Since then we have practised Nudism regularly—outdoors when the weather has been suitable, and indoors when it has been inclement.

A fellow member of one of our clubs, an Australasian—a big, well-built man who looked to be about fifty years of age, although actually over sixty—told me that in his childhood it was usual for him to bathe with his brothers and sisters in a river running through their farm. They used to undress in the house and then run down to the water completely nude. When they reached adolescence, however, they developed a certain amount of self-consciousness, probably induced from outside sources, and the girls and youths used to take their bathing separately. No costumes were worn either for river or sea-bathing, and they all used to delight in the freedom of a sun-bath. For some years he practised as a gymnastic instructor, sun- and air-bathing in the nude whenever opportunity offered; but in later life he reached a weight of 17st. and felt himself getting out of condition. He took up exercises and sun- and surf-bathing again, and reduced his weight to 12st. 2lbs. To prove that he really had regained youth and health, he shipped from Auckland, N.Z., in the engine-room of a steamer and arrived in London perfectly fit and "as hard as nails." Considering that he must have been over fifty years of age at the time, it was a really remarkable "come-back." In England and America he missed his previous opportunities for nude bathing and sun-bathing. He said that in the open-air baths in Sydney, N.S.W., provision was made for nude sun-bathing on two raised but enclosed platforms (one for men and one for women), and there were many places along the coast where a quiet spot could be found for nude bathing. It was nearly ten years from the occasion of his last sun-bath before he learnt of a Nudist club, which he then joined with great satisfaction. He now looks a picture of health and at least ten years younger than his age.

One young man told me that he gained his first experience of Nudism in South Africa. He had been keen on keeping himself fit by boxing, skipping and general exercises, and he was fond of swimming. Some friends invited him to their bathing pool, where they swam and sun-bathed without costumes, and one morning he went to this pool—a basin in the rocks, partly natural and partly hewn, on the coast. He did not quite like the idea of bathing nude in company (although they were all of the male sex), but returned later in the morning expecting to find the pool deserted. It was, except for an elderly man lying naked upon a towel and sun-bathing. After a few minutes' consideration my friend decided that if it was good enough for the old gentleman it was good enough for him, so he stripped off his clothes, dived in, and after a swim and a little skipping, lay down on the rocks himself as naked as his neighbour. He enjoyed his experience so much that he became a regular visitor at the pool, and often he bathed and sun-bathed in the nude in the little coves and beaches around the coast. He had no experience of mixed Nudism until he returned to England, when he joined a Nudist club. He is now fortunate enough to possess a large and secluded garden of his own in which he can play and work without worrying about wearing clothes.

Another young man was interested in the Scout movement, especially camping. Owing to a nervous breakdown he was advised by his doctor to "take things easy" and to give up his evening work with the Scouts, which had been somewhat strenuous. He did not want to give up camping, but felt he was not justified in enjoying the benefits of the Scouts' camp when he was no longer working in their behalf. A very con-scientious young man, it will be observed. He investigated some camping clubs, but did not like them on account of the artificial atmosphere with which they were imbued. Then he saw an advertisement of a Nudist camp, joined it, and has been an enthusiastic Nudist ever since. On making the acquaintance of a young woman, newly joined, I was intrigued to find that she had been studying the Nudist movement for about a year when she read my book, which finally decided her to take the plunge and try it out for herself. She was quite alone when she joined, but she immediately became one of the large family and now looks forward to her Sunday in camp as the event of the week.

I had the privilege of transporting one couple from the railway station to the camp on their first visit, and I could see that in spite of their apparent good spirits they were bordering on a state of "nerves." I completely ignored this and treated them as if they were members of old standing, without any open attempt to put them at their ease with the result that they arrived at the camp with every appearance of sang-froid. They told me afterwards, however, that on reaching the clearing their courage nearly failed them and they wished themselves at home again. Everyone treated them as old friends, and by lunch-time they were thoroughly at home and enjoying themselves immensely. Although a visit involves over two hours' travelling each way, they have been regular attendants at the camp ever since and they say they know of nothing more enjoyable. As a contrast, one friend brought a young lady with him on another occasion and she showed not the slightest embarrassment. She was athletic, well-read and generally charming. On arrival she went with my wife into our tent and they came out together undressed, one just as much at home as the other. I could hardly believe that this was her first experience of the kind, but she assured me that it was and she could not see anything to get excited about. It seemed quite a matter of course to her.

One young engaged couple who had done a lot of sun-bathing in swimming costumes saw an advertisement of a man and wife inviting a young couple to join them in sunbathing at their bungalow. They answered the advertisement, met the advertiser at a small village in Surrey and were taken home to tea. There was a small swimming pool in the garden and the host invited them to join in a dip, explaining that he and his wife and little daughter bathed without costumes, but the visitors could please themselves. They followed the example of their host and realised for the first time the advantages of bathing without clinging, clammy costumes. Afterwards they spent a number of very happy week-ends at their host's bungalow near Rye Harbour, and eventually went with him and his wife to a woodland club. They became confirmed Nudists and are now members of a club near London with both indoor and outdoor facilities. Another man was engaged in a Government Department when, in the course of his duties, he came in contact with some copies of an American Nudist magazine. He was interested and spent a short holiday with his small son at a seaside resort where nude sun-bathing was possible. Then he joined a regular club, and his wife, after one visit, decided to accompany him.

I can only give a few examples, but from the foregoing it will be seen that Nudists are recruited from all classes for all sorts of reasons. Many have found it difficult to give me any really concrete reason other than that they always "liked to be without clothes" whenever possible. In the case of ladies, they have generally been introduced by friends, either lady or gentleman. Not unnaturally, perhaps, they seem to be more convinced by lady members than by gentlemen. Although books and magazines may have a great deal to do with forming definite opinions on the subject, I think in most cases the inclination to be free from clothes in the sun and air has been more or less inherent though latent. Indeed, in my experience, it seems that this freedom is just a natural desire in most people suppressed through training and environment. All parents know that small children love to be naked and are only prevented from shedding their clothes irresponsibly by instruction and supervision. Again, although I have met a number of people, of both sexes, who have regarded their initiation as somewhat of an ordeal, in nearly every case the doubts and fears have been the result of introspection and imagination, and dispelled immediately upon coming into contact with the realities.

I feel I should not conclude this chapter without reference to Mrs. Marian Lili, the indefatigable Secretary of the National Sun and Air Association. I believe she was the first woman in England to practise Nudism in mixed company. She has told me that the movement really started at the Welsh Harp, Hendon, some ten years ago, when a small band of men decided to bathe without costumes. Subsequently it was decided to invite a few ladies to join them, one of whom was Marian Lili, whose husband was already a member of the original group. She went, and she found several ladies all wearing costumes, but as she had come prepared to be a real Nudist she decided to go through with it and divested herself of all clothing and took the water completely naked. Her example was soon followed by the other ladies, and this group formed the nucleus of a Society which subsequently became known to the world as "The National Sun and Air Association." Needless to say, she is bringing up her three little daughters as wholehearted Nudists, and all who have seen pictures of them in the daily Press will agree that she has cause to be proud of them.

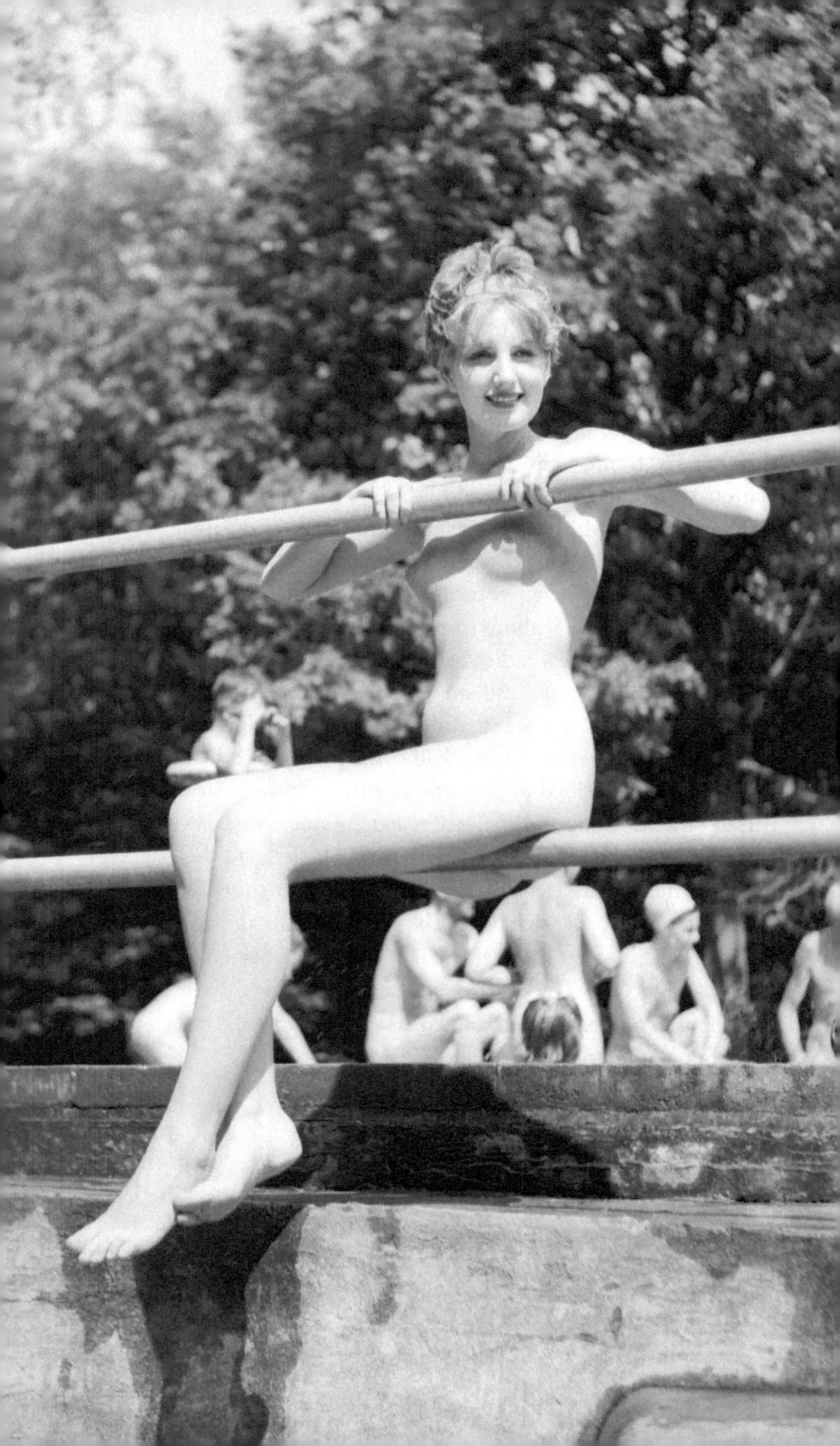

CHAPTER VI

Clubs We Have Visited and My "Ideal" Club

I HOPE YOU will have noticed that I have headed this chapter "Clubs We Have Visited." Although I was prepared to undergo my initiation on my own responsibility and without moral support, my wife decided that she would "steel" herself to the ordeal and accompany me. Since then, I have never even contemplated a visit without her. The only occasion on which I lacked her moral support was when, about seven years ago, I made my first and abortive investigation of a Nudist club.

As I have explained in the preceding chapter, I was drawn to Nudism by the highly satisfactory results of sun-bathing experiments in my own garden, and having noticed an advertisement constantly recurring in a weekly periodical, I wrote for more detailed particulars. The prospectus was excellent. Having spent some twenty-five years in the business of Advertising, I regard myself as a good judge of "copy," and I am sure I could not have written this prospectus more effectively had I been commissioned to do so in my professional capacity. Those who are acquainted with advertising men will realise the significance of such an admission. Unfortunately, personal investigation

Left: *Perched at the Poolside.*

did not justify the optimism engendered by the prospectus. I found the Secretary's office in a small suburban house, in not too good a state of repair, and was kept waiting for about half-an-hour while two other "prospects" were interviewed. When my turn came, I was ushered into a small room somewhat crowded with furniture and a central table littered with Nudist magazines. I explained that I sought an opportunity of sunning myself during the winter, and that although I had a "lamp," it was not as powerful as I could wish and I found it rather boring to sit in front of it by myself, unable to read because of the goggles and enjoying complete isolation in my bedroom. I thought it would be delightful to play games and chat with sympathetic spirits in an atmosphere irradiated by artificial sunlight, just as though it were still summer-time. But I was curious as to how this could be effected. If the artificial rays were strong enough to prove beneficial, one would, presumably, have to wear darkened goggles to protect the eyes, and I could not quite visualise a game of Badminton under these conditions. How was it worked? Was there a powerful "sun-ray" lamp at each corner of the room, or strips of quartz glass tubing containing mercury vapour run round the cornice? And what form of heating was employed? My host looked at me as though I was somewhat of an eccentric and explained that the "Nudarium" was illuminated by ordinary electric light bulbs and heated by means of a coal-fire. I was distinctly dashed. He endeavoured to reassure me by saying that a "sun-ray" lamp was provided for those requiring "treatment" at a small charge per treatment. I was interested. What type of lamp? Was it a quartz or mercury lamp or carbon arc? The reply was that it was "a proper 'sun-ray' lamp—just like real sunlight," and I began to realise that he knew far less about artificial sunlight than I did myself. Apparently most of his clients were indifferent or ignorant regarding the various types of lamp, and this was quite a side-issue. I asked how many, approximately, members he had, and the reply was astounding. "I haven't the faintest idea! Probably hundreds." I was shown a small amateur photograph of "a corner of the Nudarium," which appeared to be a sort of cubicle enclosed by ply-wood partitions, and when I asked if I could inspect the premises—not, of course, when in use by members, but at some unoccupied time—I was told: "Not under any circumstances whatever!" Finally, I asked what was the procedure if I did decide to join, and I was told that I could send along a subscription and I should receive full instructions as to the address ("somewhere in the West-End") and could go along at once. I did not join. This was different from anything I had expected, and I came to the conclusion that Nudism might be all right on the Continent, but was out of place in England.

I am glad to say that subsequent experiences proved that I was wrong. For the time being I gave up all idea of participating in Nudism actively (unless I could make a trip to Germany or France) but I continued my interest in the subject and, arising out of various discussions, I wrote *Naked and Unashamed*. This, as I said in my Introduction, "is not intended to be used as a text-book by students. Nor is it a tract to be used as propaganda either for or against Nudism." It was a consideration of the subject from the Historical, Moral, Health, Psychological, Aesthetic and Commonsense points of view which would enable the reader to judge for himself (or herself) the merits of the movement. The book was an immediate success and brought me letters from all over the world. One was an invitation from Mr. J. W. Joseph to visit the New Forest Club. The letter was sincere and gave an impression of soundness. As I have said, I was prepared to act according to my convictions and had but slight qualms regarding my initiation. When my wife said that if I was going she would come too, I pointed out that we should probably be expected to discard our clothing and appear in the "altogether" like the rest of the community, and she began to vacillate. Could she wear a bathing costume? I did not know, but would ask Mr. Joseph. His reply was that she could wear what she liked, but he was confident that she would soon want to be like the others. We were received by Mr. Joseph at his charming home set in the verge of the New Forest, and after a few minutes' chat, taken along to the club. After parking the car, we were led to a high door with a Yale lock, and as the door clicked behind us, I, at least, felt we were in a new world. The die was cast; we had taken the irrevocable step. I may say that I carried a small attache case in which reposed a bathing costume for my wife and a pair of swimming shorts for myself in case we should feel unequal to "going the whole hog" at the last moment. They were never used. As we stood on the steps of the pavilion a lady, wearing nothing but a broad sun-hat, came up and was introduced as our host's wife. I had thought that where all were nude there would be no feeling of embarrassment, but for the nude and the clothed to meet called for a greater degree of sang-froid than most people possess. To my subsequent surprise, I did not think of it at all at the time, there was not the slightest trace of embarrassment in any of us. Here was a man fully clothed introducing a husband and wife, hardly known to him, also fully clothed, to his wife, who was entirely naked. We, who had never seen an unclothed person of the opposite sex other than one another met nakedness in a social setting, so to speak, and . . . it all seemed perfectly natural. Mr. Joseph and his wife are charming people. It was, perhaps, owing to this, even more than our own dispositions, that we felt at home immediately; and when Mr. Joseph asked his wife to take mine to the ladies' dressing-room, the latter walked off with complete nonchalance; and when next I saw her, she was sitting in a deck-chair completely nude and animatedly chatting with her hostess as though she had been used to such situations all her life. The bathing costumes were forgotten.

The New Forest Club, opened in May, 1934, developed rapidly. Although situated in a picturesque woodland, it was provided with Company's water, gas and electric light. Hot meals were served at mid-day and in the evening, and a bath-hut was installed with hot and cold water supplies. In 1936 a still more ambitious step was taken. A large house with extensive grounds was acquired near Bournemouth. The "new" New Forest Club is really like a first-class hotel (although huts and chalets in the grounds can be rented by those preferring the "simple life") and food and service are excellent. One end of the grounds has a sea frontage of 400 feet, and although it is not permissible to bathe in the sea itself without some form of costume, a natural swimming pool inside the grounds is replenished with fresh sea-water at each tide. So real sea-bathing in the nude is actually available. On our way home, my wife, who had been very dubious as to how she would feel when the "psychological moment" arrived, said: "I have made up my mind! We must start a club of our own!" I was rather taken aback at this complete reversal of her previous attitude, but agreed that I, too, felt like that. I pointed out, however, that it was not quite so simple as it might seem. Questions of finance, responsibility and method would need to be very carefully considered, and it was out of this consideration and subsequent discussions that this chapter was evolved. Much water has flowed under the bridges since then, and we have visited many clubs and gained a good deal of experience. As a result, I offer my ideas to those who contemplate forming a Nudist Club, and even those who are now running such clubs may find some of my suggestions helpful, or at least provocative of thought.

The first thing to consider, I think, is the constitution of the club. At present there are three different forms adopted. The proprietary club, conducted entirely or mainly as a financial investment; the "communistic" variety, where a number of enthusiasts combine to acquire a suitable site which individually none of them could afford; and a sort of compromise where the proprietor provides the necessary capital and takes whatever profit may accrue, while leaving the general management to a committee elected by the members themselves. In most cases these methods seem to work with equal satisfaction. Personally, I think there are drawbacks to all of them. The purely proprietary club, however sincere the proprietor, does offer opportunities of criticism by the ill-informed, who may suggest that the whole thing is a ramp or a "money-making racket." The communistic type is usually formed by enthusiasts without much capital, individually or collectively, and necessitates renting a site and providing most of the amenities by voluntary labour. Estimable as this may be in the abstract, it has many disadvantages. Primarily, insecurity of tenure is liable to cramp development. It hardly seems worth while to expend great effort in improvements and general development of the site when the tenancy may be discontinued at the will of the landlord. It more or less precludes the trouble and expense of making a swimming pool, for instance, and is likely to make the members content with "makeshift" amenities. My own feeling is that the ideal club should be a combination of proprietary and communistic. I consider it essential that the site, or premises, should belong to the club, and this requires that sufficient capital shall be available for purchase. Such capital cannot be raised merely by subscriptions. Many clubs nowadays insist upon entrance fees, and I believe that if instead of entrance fees a purchase of shares could be arranged, capital could be provided and the club formed on a co-operative or profit-sharing basis. I know there are difficulties. I am not a financier, but I am convinced that these difficulties could be overcome.

I regard this question of capital as of vital importance and consider it essential that reasonable amenities should be provided at the outset. The mere provision of a piece of ground where it is possible to discard clothing is, in my opinion, not worthy of being called a club and offers very little attraction to potential members. It is a vicious circle. Amenities cannot be provided without money, money will not be forthcoming without subscriptions, and subscriptions will not be offered without amenities to attract them. Of course, it is not likely that the desideratum would be achieved right away. Amenities cost money, and money could scarcely be expected to flow in until something concrete could be shown in the way of security. The articles of association would have to provide for the devotion of a good proportion of capital *and income* to general improvements. Obviously, the initial capital would have to be provided by a nucleus of shareholders with definite plans for development as the funds available increased.

This brings us to the consideration of what an ideal club might offer, realising, of course, that development would take place *pari passu* with increase of income. First must be found a suitable site. This should be woodland composed mainly of small trees and thickets to afford satisfactory screening from the public. Not less than five acres should be available, with possibilities of extension. Some clubs are screened by wattled hurdles or woven board fencing, but I regard this as unsatisfactory inasmuch as it is a sort of advertisement that something is being hidden behind them and it is likely to arouse curiosity and suspicion. If the woodland is fairly thick, I would run strands of barbed wire *just inside the boundary,* where it would be inconspicuous from a little distance, and then inside this I would fill up gaps and thin sections with underbrush. If necessary, in places I would use hurdles or woven boards *inside* this, so that the inner parts of the wood would be secure from outside observation without any special protection being noticeable by the passer-by. If the freehold were acquired it would be quite worth while to plant a belt of quick-growing trees and shrubs near the outer barrier. In the centre would be one large clearing suitable for community games and exercises, with smaller clearings for badminton or ring-tennis courts. Although a soft, springy lawn is delightful to play on barefooted, it will not stand continual trampling by crowds of people, and so I would have the exercise ground and courts liable to hard wear covered with a few inches of fine sand which could be raked smooth and even periodically. A pavilion of pleasing appearance large enough to shelter a good number of members in bad weather with a suitable form of heating would be provided, together with a buffet for tea and other refreshments. Separate dressing-rooms for ladies and gentlemen would be available in this building.

A swimming pool is almost a *sine qua non*, and provision should be made for this when laying out the site, even though the initial funds were insufficient for immediate construction. Shower and foot-baths would be a natural corollary of the swimming pool, but pending the provision of the latter, simple shower-baths could be constructed with very little trouble and expense, provided a suitable water supply were available, and this, indeed, may be considered as one of the essentials of any Nudist club. Members should be allowed facilities for erecting small huts or tents, and it would be an advantage for the club to have one or two of these which could be let to members who preferred hiring to purchasing their own. These should provide a useful addition to the club's revenue. Another essential is suitable sanitary accommodation. The ordinary form of camp latrine is repellent to a great many people, and as the club should encourage the spending of holidays on the premises, weatherproof huts fitted with "Elsan" appliances should be available—one for ladies and one for gentlemen. These should be placed in secluded positions approached by screened paths, at the entrance of which a board should be hung upon a tree or stake, bearing upon one side "VACANT" and on the other "ENGAGED." This board would be reversed upon entering and leaving the path.

In addition to classes in physical culture, members will require some more entertaining forms of exercise, and here there is plenty of scope. Badminton, played with outdoor shuffles (with rubber instead of cork bases to steady them in currents of air) or with little woolly balls, is both amusing and invigorating. "Tennikoit" or Ring Tennis is always popular among skilled and unskilled alike, and is a good healthy exercise. Lawn Tennis is a great attraction if the resources of the club permit the construction of grass or "hard" courts. "Miniten" is an ingenious adaptation of lawn tennis for a small court. It is played with "bats" made from two discs of ply-wood about nine inches in diameter, fastened together at an angle by a small strip of wood which serves as a handle (somewhat in the form of a wooden gauntlet) and an uncovered rubber ball a little larger than an ordinary tennis ball. Medicine Balls of varying weights are almost an essential of the well-found Nudist club, although an ordinary Soccer football serves as well for less strenuous members. Archery is by no means an obsolete sport, and is very suitable for Nudists.

Some fine pictures may be made by amateur photographers of amateur toxophilites, poses with the bow giving excellent effects. Bull Board as played aboard ship by throwing little circular bags filled with sand upon a board with numbered squares, needs but a very small outlay to make an effective game. Clock Golf is popular and inexpensive. Indoors (during bad weather) Table Tennis, Darts, Chess, Draughts, Dominoes, Cards, and even "Shove-ha'penny," help to pass the time pleasantly. The above are only a few of the many forms of entertainment suitable for a Nudist club, and readers will, doubtless, be able to lengthen the list as desired; but I do think that having attracted members to a club it is desirable to give them every possible facility for healthy enjoyment.

Although a Nudist, I do not subscribe to the "Back-to-Nature" philosophy. I believe in making things as comfortable and gay as possible while enjoying the freedom offered by a sun-and-air bath. There should be a plentiful supply of deck-chairs and sun-lounges, and the canvases of these should be bright and cheerful. Wind-shelters made from gaily-striped awnings might add still further to the effect.

No club can be complete without members. The selection of these is all-important, not less so than the selection of the site itself. "Subscriptions at all costs" is a policy doomed to failure and, perhaps, catastrophe. In this connection there is the problem of applications from single men without a partner of the opposite sex. There are some clubs which refuse to entertain such applications at all; others which demand a heavily-increased subscription for a single man. The first I regard as arbitrary and undesirable; the second as a rather feeble compromise. I believe that in some of the clubs in Germany, France and America the fees are exactly the same for either sex. Perhaps the movement is not sufficiently advanced here to make this possible; but I should like to see it tried out. It is reasonable to make a reduction for married or engaged couples, because in these cases the whole of the cost usually falls upon the man. As regards single men, I think such cases should be decided upon their merits by a committee of club members. There must be thousands of fine, clean-living young men, interested in physical culture and a healthy outdoor life, who have no fiancées or girlfriends with whom they are sufficiently well acquainted to propose a joint subscription to a Nudist club.

All clubs must have rules, but I should make these as simple as possible with a minimum of "verbotens." They would be so framed that all decent people would automatically agree with them without feeling harshly restricted. I would ban alcohol, but not tobacco. Members would be either nude or segregated to an enclosure where trunks, slips and brassieres or bathing costumes were worn. Genuine, proved Nudist members would be permitted to don shorts or wraps when the weather was chilly or in the early morning or evening, but semi-undress would be regarded as an impropriety, and all dressing and undressing would be confined to the dressing-rooms. Photographs would be taken only when those likely to be included in the picture had definitely expressed their approval and any use of prints for commercial purposes would require special permission from the Committee.

I would allow members of good standing to bring as guests prospective members for whom they could vouch, without any charge whatever; but I would see that this privilege was not abused. Every week-end or public holiday, when a large number of members might be expected to congregate, at least one member of the Committee would be on duty as Warden and all new members would be met at the entrance, by a fully-clothed member, and afterwards informally introduced to the community. I would take every possible precaution to sift applications for membership, but once elected I would use every effort to make each member feel welcome and perfectly at home. With the exception of the physical exercises, there would be no "organised" recreations. Games would be left to individual selection and friendly arrangement. I think the German "systemisation" unsuitable to English temperament.

This is but a very bare outline of my idea of an "ideal club," and many of its features are already in existence in some clubs; but some of them will be new to some readers and, as I said at the beginning of this chapter, at least provocative of thought which may lead to still better organisation. Actually I have described my ideals only so far as they are simple and practical. If I were to give rein to my imagination I should go much further.

Our next invitation was to attend the Conference of the National Sun and Air Association, held by the courtesy of Mrs. Bedingfield at the Lotus Club, N. Finchley. This was most interesting, as delegates came from clubs in all parts of the country, and the amazing variation in type made one realise what a widespread movement Nudism had become in England. The meetings were held in the grounds of the Club, with the table and chairs for the Chairman and his lady Secretary set under a cedar tree. I was rather amused, at first, to see a nude chairman presiding over a meeting with most of the audience reclining on the ground in a state of naked-ness—especially as the proceedings were conducted with the formality and solemnity characteristic of an old-fashioned political or even religious meeting. I had received a shock, too, when ascending to the dressing-room I encountered two young men tripping down the stairs completely unclothed. I had scarcely considered the possibilities of indoor Nudism, and as I looked through a doorway and saw a nude violinist accompanied by a nude pianist, I did feel a little like "Alice in Wonderland." Nakedness in the woods under shining sun and blue sky seemed perfectly natural, but nakedness indoors was another matter. We soon grew used to it, however, when we noticed how perfectly at ease all the other visitors were. And there were about 150 of them altogether. As the sun descended it began to get a bit chilly, and there was some laughter as a young girl dashed into the house and came out with a couple of rugs—one for herself and one for the young man beside her. Soon after, most of us sought shelter in the house from the keen wind which blew up, and we settled down to tea in a large lounge with a cheerful fire blazing in the grate. I was impressed with the general friendliness of the company. Complete strangers seemed to drop into engrossing conversations and discussions as easily as if they were members of one family, and I suppose that, in a sense, was what they were. Some of the resolutions proposed (and carried) at the meeting were rather ambitious and I doubt if many of them will be realised, at least for some years to come; but "Unity is Strength," and I think the feeling of mutual support induced an optimism and assurance which otherwise would have been lacking.

We met and talked with so many people that we came away with our minds confused, but we had arranged to pay a further visit to the "Lotus" the following week to see what it was like under normal conditions. "Lotus" members formed but a small proportion of the gathering during the Conference.

On our next visit to the "Lotus" we found quite a different atmosphere. All the members seemed old friends and we felt "at home" immediately. As the weather was uninviting we had our first experience of entirely indoor Nudism. We helped ourselves to a variety of sandwiches, all fresh and dainty, and the charming young lady in charge served us with tea. We chatted with our neighbours freely and they all seemed above the average in interest and intelligence. Believing that one of the main objects of Nudism is untrammelled exercise, we adjourned to the "Sports Room" for a game of Badminton. Neither of us are expert or experienced players; but the "all in" rules were a revelation. The room is not big enough for an orthodox court, so these rules were conceived by some ingenious individual to make a spirited game possible. If the shuttlecock hits the ceiling, the walls, or curtains at either end, it is taken on the rebound as if it had come direct from the opposing player. According to these rules it is permissible to catch the shuttle on the racquet, bounce it and return it. All sorts of complications ensue which might exacerbate a real player, but are quite enjoyable for those who seek fun and exercise. Here also we experienced the delight of playing table-tennis free from clothing, and enjoyed it so much that we later had a table made for use at home and became fairly enthusiastic players. Only those who have played this game strenuously can have any idea of the amount of exertion involved, and the constant stooping to pick up balls is in itself a. form of physical culture. Which leads me to our first experience of "physical jerks." Later in the evening a call was raised for the "beginners' class." My wife and I, with other members, returned to the Sports room, which had been cleared for action, and found an assembly of about twenty persons of all ages and both sexes. Our Mentor was a young and feminine counterpart of a Guards instructor. It soon became obvious that this was a serious matter, and while her vocabulary lacked the spice and picturesqueness of that of an Army sergeant, it was incisive and all-embracing. She herself appeared to be made of whale-bone, and I am afraid the ease with which she performed the exercises made it difficult for her to realise that some of the apparent slackers were really doing their best. For myself, I was rather too conscientious and suffered considerably during the next few days. I have since formed very definite opinions as to the qualifications of a physical culture instructor and have decided that zeal should be tempered with discretion. Nevertheless, we enjoyed ourselves so much that before leaving we enrolled as regular members, and we have never had any cause to regret our decision.

At the Conference we became acquainted with an enthusiast in the neighbourhood of sixty years of age, but with the liveliness and agility of a vigorous schoolboy, and we received from him an invitation to visit his club near Windsor. Soon afterwards we met him, by appointment, at Waterloo and proceeded to Windsor. It was a miserable day. Leaden skies and steadily soaking rain were enough to damp the enthusiasm, literally, of any but the very keen. Our somewhat elderly friend, however, had sufficient vim for all of us, and we soon became infected by his sprightliness. Arrived at Windsor, we did a little shopping in the way of fruit and other comestibles, and then boarded a motor-bus which deposited us within a mile or so of our destination. After a long walk up a road that was little more than a cart-track, we reached a farm, and above this, on a wooded hillside, lay the camp. It really was a camp because, with the exception of a communal but where various odds and ends were dumped, the only accommodation consisted of tents. We were lucky. Our friend introduced us to a lady who owned (with her husband, who was a Nature

Doctor) a large and almost luxurious tent. Here we lunched and spent most of the afternoon. We saw little of the other members, of whom very few were present, and although our friend offered to disrobe if I wished to "go Nudist," we saw nothing even suggestive of Nudism. I can imagine, however, that this camp, high on the side of a hill with a carpet of pine needles underfoot and its pure bracing air, would be ideal on a hot summer day.

Our next visit was to "Yew Tree Camp," the sun-bathing "park" of the "Sun-bathing Society." After a steady climb through some steep woodland we arrived at a gate and a sort of lodge-hut, the door of which (after our ringing a loud bell) was opened by an amiable young lady, fully clothed. We were requested to fill in a form containing a sort of questionnaire which was almost like the "third degree" in print, and were then taken to the dressing-rooms. The Sunbathing Society is one of the veteran clubs, and I believe that at its inception it was *de rigueur* for the men to wear trunks and the ladies to wear slips and brassieres. Theoretically, complete nudity is confined to the "family enclosure," but we saw only one lady in the original uniform, and the only other form of clothing was that of a gentleman who was introduced to us by the lady secretary (who in the meantime had doffed her frock) and who was somewhat unconventionally clad in a sports jacket and nothing else. Again we found friendliness and interesting people to talk to. We did not join in any of the games, but we amused ourselves with a medicine ball and envied the members disporting themselves in the swimming pool. We did not indulge in a "splash" ourselves, partly because the day was overcast and chilly, but more particularly because we had not provided ourselves with towels. Our acquaintance in the sports jacket introduced us to his wife and told us, in a rather amusing way, how they became members. A neighbour and his wife, with whom our friends regularly played bridge, had induced the gentleman to accompany him to the "park" to see for himself what it was like, and although he agreed rather reluctantly, he enjoyed himself so much that he decided to become a member providing his wife was willing to accompany him. The wife was positively horrified by the idea, but after many discussions at the bridge parties, was eventually persuaded to make a trial. At the "park" he introduced her to one or two people and left her for a few minutes while he had a look round. When he returned she was all alone and looking a picture of misery. All she wanted to know was how soon they could go home! He argued that she had not yet given it a fair trial and got her to chat with one or two more members, and when she seemed to be settling down to it more happily he left her again. On his second return he found her so engrossed in animated conversation with two gentlemen that she hardly took any notice of him, and from then onwards she became an ardent enthusiast. They spent their summer holidays at a Nudist holiday centre in Devonshire. There was no indoor accommodation at "Yew Tree Camp," so as the sun sank and we found it getting even more chilly, we returned to the dressing-rooms, donned our clothes, and said good-bye with the hope, mutually expressed, that we should soon meet again. We noticed several tents and learnt that quite a few of the members made a practice of spending their summer holidays at the camp under canvas.

Until now, all the Clubs with which we had been in touch
were, with the exception of the "Lotus," too far away from
home to justify our becoming members, and we searched,
for a time in vain, for an Essex club. We had heard, vaguely,
of the "Diogenes" and other clubs near St. Albans, Herts.;
but our own county seemed "off the map" so far as Nudism
was concerned. And then we were introduced to "The Essex
Sparta." Here we found, after a tramp across three big fields,
a wood of about 12½ acres with a fair-sized central clearing.
We were introduced to the members present, about a couple
of dozen, by our Christian names, and endeavoured, more or
less unsuccessfully, to remember theirs. This system of iden-
tification becomes rather complicated when there are two or
three Erics, three or four Johns, and several Bills and Bobs.
They were a jolly crowd and soon made us feel at home. I
enjoyed the thrill of seeing one lady member absorbed in my
book with two young men also reading it over her shoulder.
We played ring tennis and were taken for a tour through the
woods by the Secretary and other members, and we voted it
charming. By the time we had to get ready for our return we
had decided to become members, and we arranged to come
back on the following Sunday with our three children. This
we did, and although it was their first experience, the children
took to it "like ducks to water." We became so enthusiastic
that the following day we bought a small sectional garage to
serve as our woodland home and I planned out various fixtures
and fittings, including a locker-seat, shelves and similar conveniences. We found willing hands to help us erect the but
when it arrived, and we laid in a stock of crockery and cooking
equipment with a view to spending some of our summer

holidays on the spot. We already had two tents which the children used when sleeping in the garden at home. Fate was against us. Bad weather prevented us from getting very far with our preparations, and at the end of the year the farm was sold and the new owner refused to renew the lease under which the site was held by the Club.

In the meantime, we had attended the reopening of the "Gymnic" Club, an entirely indoor organisation, although members were offered facilities for visiting one of the outdoor clubs near St. Albans. Being in the nature of a "reunion," everyone seemed in high spirits and games were organised in the room set apart for sports and exercises. This was really two rooms made into one as the house (situated near Olympia) was of the large old-fashioned type in which the ground and first floors consist of two rooms divided by folding doors. The "games" were of the children's party variety, but they induced great activity and hilarity, and were followed by even the middle-aged with great keenness. Two sides, each consisting of an equal number of both sexes, were chosen by the two captains, and, to begin with, they sat on the polished floor with legs stretched out in front in opposed ranks. Then one "umpire" dropped an air balloon between them and each team tried, with the use of only one hand and legs kept on the floor, to strike the balloon over the heads of their opponents. If it touched the ground on the other side, it scored a "goal." Another competition consisted in a sort of relay-race in which one gentleman balanced a balloon on a plate, ran the length of the room and handed the plate and balloon to a lady awaiting it, who, in her turn, ran back and transferred it to the next gentleman, and so on until the whole line had participated, the winning side being that which completed the sequence first. These and some of the other games played might seem a little childish in cold blood, but the excitement was maintained to a remarkable degree and the activity of the players was a thing to wonder at. We were shown all over the club, which comprises four floors, including the basement, and is equipped with hot and cold baths and showers, and a mercury-vapour lamp which emits powerful ultra-violet rays, supplemented by the infra-red rays of a bulb lamp fixed above it.

Having, by this time, become acclimatised to "indoor" Nudism, we experienced no surprise when one of the Sparta members invited those for whom it was convenient to meet weekly at his house for general discussions, and after one or two meetings an excellent physical culture instructor was introduced who gave us an hour's training each week with very excellent effect. I have to thank him for fitness during the winter months which otherwise I never should have enjoyed. As spring advanced it was decided to discontinue these weekly meetings, notwithstanding the willingness of our generous host to continue his hospitality; but immediately after this, two members who had been energetically searching for a new site were successful in finding a charming little wood of about six acres. It was a fairly thick wood composed of small oaks, ash, beech, and quite large hawthorns. On our first visit we were shown "where the clearing will be"; but it all looked the same to us, and we nearly lost ourselves in trying to find a way to get out. The following week-end a marvellous transformation took place. Trees were topped and the toppings dragged to the boundary to fill up weak spots; then the trees were cut down, and finally the roots dug out. I think the members who contributed so energetically to this work (I may say that my family and I took a share in it) would have shocked any Trade Union with their hours and their vigour. By Whitsun we had a clearing larger than that of the old camp, three huts erected and the boundaries fairly well consolidated. On leaving the original site I had had my own hut brought home, where I completed my fittings and finished up with painting it inside and out, and as the camp site was only rented and I found transport a very expensive item where huts were concerned, I decided to purchase a tent for my wife and myself, which could be used for us to sleep in and as a rendezvous for the family in case of bad weather. The children had their own tents for sleeping in, supplemented by fly-sheets which I had specially made for use away from home. Our first night was almost a tragedy. We had not had time to get everything properly organised and whenever we wanted anything we had to move almost everything else to find it. About three o'clock in the morning my wife and I were unable to sleep for the cold, in spite of our sleeping-bags. I put on a pair of flannel trousers and a jersey (over my pyjamas) and my wife piled some clothes on the outside of her sleeping-bag. Then the storm broke, and between flashes of lightning and crashes of thunder we listened to the rain falling down in sheets. Our tent, with a fly-sheet, kept perfectly dry, but we found in the morning that the two smaller children (whose fly-sheet had not been fixed) had been nearly washed out, and my elder son in a small tent by himself had had a rivulet diverted by a small furrow into the head of his tent. With the morning sun and a mixed odour of wood-smoke and bacon frizzling over the camp-fire, we soon forgot our troubles and enjoyed a hearty meal. Needless to say, we were better prepared for the next night, and although it rained heavily, we were all quite comfortable. At the end of the season this camp was given up, but subsequently a woodland site of about eight acres was secured near Billericay and the freehold was acquired. This is a delightful spot and the original camp has now developed into a sort of colony. Our own but has been added to and improved until we may justifiably describe it as a bungalow. The walls are lined with plywood (panelled with mouldings) and distempered; a coal-stove has been installed and a full-size double bed "built in." Altogether there are now some thirty hut-bungalows owned by members and mostly occupied by families. Several parties spend regular week-ends there all through the year, and last winter some actually played in the snow entirely nude. When we look back on our early camping days we sometimes wonder whether we are not getting almost too luxurious for "simple-lifers," but we realise that discomfort is not a necessary feature of a natural and healthy life and we continue to add to our amenities.

When we visited the "White House Sun, Air and Sports Club," the lady and gentleman Directors who received us were at some pains to impress upon us that it was not actually a Nudist club, but a residential club offering facilities for sun-bathing in little or no costume, according to taste. The club-house itself has accommodation for some thirty guests so far as sleeping is concerned, and many more for meals and a number of sleeping-huts distributed in the extensive grounds. As the house is set on a steep hillside (approached from the private road which leads to it by two long flights of steps) the playing courts are on different levels and a certain amount of modest mountaineering is encountered in reaching them. The swimming pool was quite the best we had seen, and measured 45 feet by 25 feet, and we were informed that it was flood-lit by night. After being closed for some time, the "White House" has recently been reopened under entirely new management, and although I have not yet re-visited it, the fact that it is amalgamated with the "New Forest Club" persuades me that it must be well organised and likely to appeal to a very high-class membership.

Since the first edition of the book was published I have received invitations to visit various other clubs, including the "Spielplatz," near St. Albans, and the "Sunfolk" in the same district. The former has plenty of space in the woods and a large swimming pool, but seemed to lack the home-liness and camaraderie of the average club. What struck me most at the "Sunfolk" was the thoroughness with which the club had been planned and organised. The club buildings were roomy and convenient and exceedingly well kept. A communal kitchen with all conveniences was provided and water for domestic needs and the small swimming pool was pumped by a paraffin engine. Lack of space forbids my going into further details here, but I think I have said enough to give the uninitiated reader a general idea of the variety and constitution of British Nudist Clubs and the rapid progress of the movement in this country.

CHAPTER VII

Artificial Sunlight and "Indoor" Nudism

It is not surprising that the first of all religions was sun-worship. To primitive man the source of all life and heat was the sun, and it is difficult for us, with so many means of heating and lighting our homes, to realise how much the sun must have meant in those early days to our somewhat child-like ancestors, who had to endure the fear of darkness and the misery of cold when the sun had set. Actually, primitive man was not so very far from the mark because all light, with the exception of electric light, is derived from the sun. The first artificial light was, presumably, a wood fire made from vegetable fibres which had absorbed the rays of the sun, without which they could not have existed. Coal fires and gas-lighting, again, were produced from primeval vegetation which had stored up sun-energy for, perhaps, millions of years. Every schoolboy knows that moonlight is simply the light of the sun reflected from the surface of the moon. Photo-therapy, the cure of disease by sunlight, was employed by the Babylonians, Assyrians and Greeks, but it was not used scientifically until some time in the eighteenth century. The study of light through the ages led to the experiments of Sir Isaac Newton with the prism, which proved that sunlight was composed of coloured rays. Some hundred years later, Herschel discovered that there were rays outside or beyond the edge of the visible spectrum which radiated heat, although they were invisible because they were without light. These rays became known as "infra-red," and in 1801 J. W. Ritter discovered further invisible rays at the other end of the spectrum described as "ultra-violet" rays. These rays are cold rays, but possess qualities which produce very remarkable effects. All these rays are, of course, included in natural sunlight providing they are not filtered out by intervening substances. In 1855 a Swiss doctor started an institution for curative sun-baths, and he was soon followed by doctors in other countries. It was not until 1919, however, that it was proved that rickets could be cured more rapidly by artificial ultra-violet rays than by natural sunlight. It has been found possible to procure a much greater concentration of these rays by means of an electric lamp and also to isolate them from other rays. There are two distinct types of lamp for producing artificial sunlight—the mercury vapour or "quartz lamp" which emits concentrated ultra-violet rays, and the "carbon arc" lamp which produces all rays of the visible spectrum and even the invisible ultra-violet and infra-red rays. In the first type, light is produced by passing an electric current through a quartz-glass "burner" containing mercury which is vaporised and forms an arc or flame emitting ultra-violet rays. The "burner" is made from quartz because ultra-violet rays will not penetrate ordinary glass, which acts as a filter. The property of allowing such rays to pass is the basis of "Vita glass," which can be used for windows, shelters and similar requirements. Many people fail to realise that they can sit inside a window or shelter of ordinary glass and scorch in the sun without any ultra-violet

rays reaching them at all. The carbon arc lamp does not need
to be enclosed and so there is nothing to obstruct any of the
rays emitted from the arc.

While all who have studied and experimented with sun-rays
are agreed as to the general benefits to be derived, there are two
schools of thought as to the respective merits of the "ultra-violet" and the "infra-red." Until fairly recently, the greater credit
was given to the ultra-violet. These rays cured rickets, lupus
and goitre; were most useful in non-surgical tuberculosis and
possessed general tonic qualities of real value. But eminent
men have come to the conclusion that the infra-red rays are
at least as necessary and some even claim that the infra-red are
the more valuable. Such authorities as Sir Leonard Hill, Dr.
Saleeby, Dr. Stein and Professor Dixon have pointed out that
for various reasons the infra-red rays are as necessary as the
ultra-violet. One very logical argument which can easily be
grasped by the layman is that the ultra-violet rays being very
short cannot penetrate far below the surface of the skin and
unless the blood is drawn near the surface may fail to enter the
bloodstream. And, of course, we all know the comfort of heat
for aches and pains. Hot-water bottles, hot fomentations and
poultices are regular "old wives" remedies. Without wishing
to rank myself with the great authorities on the subject, I
have studied it very carefully and it seems to me that, except
in the special treatment of particular diseases, with which we
have no concern here, ultraviolet treatment should certainly
be accompanied or supplemented by the infra-red. This, naturally, ranges me on the side of the carbon arc lamp which,
if of the right type, gives practically the equivalent of natural
sunlight. When I say "of the right type," I should perhaps

explain that a carbon arc lamp is essentially an apparatus for holding and adjusting the carbons and supplying them with suitable current. Light is formed by the carbons burning away, and when they have burned so far away from each other that the electric current will not jump across the gap, the lamp automatically ceases to function. Various devices have been invented to allow for adjustment of the carbon points so that the arc of flame is maintained. I had one lamp in which this was effected by an arrangement of electro-magnets which came into action so soon as the gap grew wide. I still have a lamp which is adjusted by hand. When the carbons burn away sufficiently to break the current, or appear to be nearing that stage, the holders are twisted in screw sockets and so brought closer together.

Here I would like to make it quite clear that insolation or irradiation at home is entirely a different matter from the treatment of definite diseases. The latter can only be under-taken by qualified medical men with powerful apparatus, which might prove positively dangerous in the hands of a layman. The dangers of "overdoing it" in natural sunlight have already been pointed out, but the danger of an overdose of ultra-violet rays is infinitely greater with a powerful mercury lamp. On the other hand, lamps sold for home use are seldom powerful enough to cure any real disease. Although carbon arc "lamps" are essentially forms of carbon holders, there is a great deal of difference in the carbons themselves. A pair of plain carbons will emit a smaller proportion of ultra-violet rays than the combination of one plain carbon with one iron-cored carbon, and there are various qualities of carbons containing other metals such as copper and tungsten. The pure tungsten carbon gives the greatest proportion of ultra-violet rays, but the carbons are very costly. There are also both carbon and metal filament incandescent lamps similar to those used for ordinary house or shop lighting, but unless the bulbs are made from special glass the ultra-violet irradiation is negligible. Baths comprising clusters of such bulbs, however, have considerable value and will induce perspiration at a very much lower temperature than a Turkish or vapour bath.

In nearly all cases where light treatment is involved, the "building up of resistance," the stimulation of the endocrine glands and the general improvement in the metabolism play a very important part, and regarded as a preventive rather than a cure, this is of the utmost importance to those who wish to keep well. It has, moreover, been proved that in foods which have been treated by ultra-violet light the Vitamin D content has been increased and there seems good reason to believe that the milk of cows and goats which have been irradiated by natural sunlight in the summer and fed upon foods so irradiated, give milk more valuable than can be obtained from these animals in the winter. It may not be generally known that cod-liver oil, so rich in vitamin D, derives its chief value from sunlight. The codfish feeds on minute organisms which have absorbed the rays of the sun and become rich in chlorophyll, that vitalising substance already referred to in an earlier chapter.

Before concluding, I should like to return to the question of the respective values of the ultra-violet and infra-red rays. Natural sunlight is composed of 75 per cent. red and infra-red rays, and since the latter have therapeutic qualities of their own and in addition improve the effects of the ultra-violet, it does seem essential that their aid should be obtained from gas-fire or electric heater, or even a coal-fire. If using a mercury-vapour lamp I would strongly recommend a general "warming-up" of the skin and self-massage by means of "rubbing" exercises before exposure to the rays of the lamp. Such action will draw the blood nearer to the surface where it may be reached by the short rays and ensure good circulation so that the beneficial effects may be carried to all parts of the system. I am also of the opinion that for general toning-up purposes the open carbon arc, whether double, triple or quadruple carbons are used, is preferable to the mercury lamp. If artificial sunlight is the goal in view it will be more nearly achieved by this means, although it is not possible to secure a perfect substitute for natural sunlight and the open air.

Allied with this subject of "Artificial Sunlight" is the question of "Indoor Nudism." There are many enthusiastic Nudists who enjoy the natural sunlight and fresh air of the camps, yet are averse to what is called "indoor" Nudism. They join Nudist clubs for sunshine and health; why should they bother about taking off their clothes indoors? But there are always two sides to every question, and although I once decried indoor Nudism myself, my wife and I became members of a club with indoor accommodation and we have spent many enjoyable hours there. Let it be under-stood at the outset that I do not claim equable comparison between outdoor and in-door Nudism. I do not think anyone does. Like artificial sunlight, it is a sub-stitute; or perhaps I should say a supplement. I do not know any members who confine them-selves to indoor Nudism. All those I have met are keen outdoor Nudists *during the outdoor season*. We hear of Spartan characters who break the ice in the

Serpentine or Highgate Ponds and bathe in the open all the year round; but such practices are not for everyone. On the snow-clad Alps, or in the Austrian Tyrol, at high altitudes with dry atmosphere and brilliant sunshine, ski-ing and skating in the nude may be enjoyed by quite average constitutions; but in the damp, dark, chilly days of winter in this country, one needs a hardy constitution and a great deal of conviction to practise Nudism in the open air. What, then, is the alternative? The most satisfactory alternative is to enjoy open-air exposure when conditions permit, and to exercise, play and generally recreate with the facilities offered *indoors* when outdoor conditions are inimical. Indoor Nudism will help the skin to carry out its natural functions. It will also encourage physical exercise with the moral stimulation of group activities.

So much for the merely physical side of the question. All Nudists agree that there is a psychological or spiritual consideration which is by no means negligible. The sensation of freedom which comes with the casting of clothes can be enjoyed just as much indoors as outdoors. The opportunity of sitting and chatting in a community of sympathetic spirits is just as welcome, once experienced. As with Nudism generally, this feeling will not apply to everyone. Just as it may be impossible for some individuals to appear nude before others without self-consciousness, so some people may not feel at ease in a roomful of people all without clothes. But such individuals are not 100 per cent. natural Nudists. Consider the simple and unwarped mind of a child. It can distinguish no difference at all between Nudism outdoors and Nudism indoors. Whatever difference an adult may perceive comes from ideas and conventions which have been built up by training and environment.

It is good for all of us to relax occasionally—to get away from the everyday rules and regulations under which most of our time is spent. The spiritual freedom of nakedness is little less refreshing than the physical freedom, and is only a logical extension of the natural instinct (in both sexes) to change into loose and informal attire for the purpose of relaxation. The shedding of clothes may be subconsciously symbolic of thrusting away all cares and worries of the daily routine; but it has a very real and practical effect. I have seen staid business and professional men develop interest and charm under the influence of such environment. I have seen middle-aged men become younger and more vigorous by playing games in the nude, which they would have considered too undignified and youthful under ordinary circumstances. And I am convinced that they have gone away from such gatherings rejuvenated and invigorated.

It is difficult for many people to understand and appreciate the enjoyment and improvement in health which may come from indoor Nudism. But then it is difficult for many people to understand and appreciate Nudism in any form at all. I think that such prejudice against indoor Nudism as exists to-day is really the residue of original prejudices against Nudism itself. The old ingrained idea that for the sexes to be grouped together without clothing must lead to immorality or the shocking of modesty, may be put to sleep while the obvious advantage to health of open air and sunshine are present, but without these easily-understood influences there is the feeling that it is not quite "right." I believe that all the people who feel like this would be convinced of their error if they once spent an evening with a group of genuine enthusiasts. In my experience, and from those of others with whom I have discussed the subject, one feels just as natural undressed indoors as outdoors; it is all a question of attitude of mind.

It is a curious fact that those who know nothing of practical Nudism imagine that the mixing of sexes without clothing must lead to and accentuate sex-consciousness, whereas those with experience know that the effect is exactly the reverse.

That the exposure of the body to sun and air is highly beneficial, physically, can be understood by most reasonable people; but the psychological benefits accruing from the mixing of the sexes without clothes needs deeper thought and a more analytical mind. I believe that any attempt to convince individuals holding aggressively antagonistic views is a mere waste of time and that the only satisfactory means of changing these views is personal, practical experience. Those broadminded enough to realise the possibility of their views being erroneous may be persuaded to make this test to satisfy themselves, and I have little doubt that it will result in self-conversion.

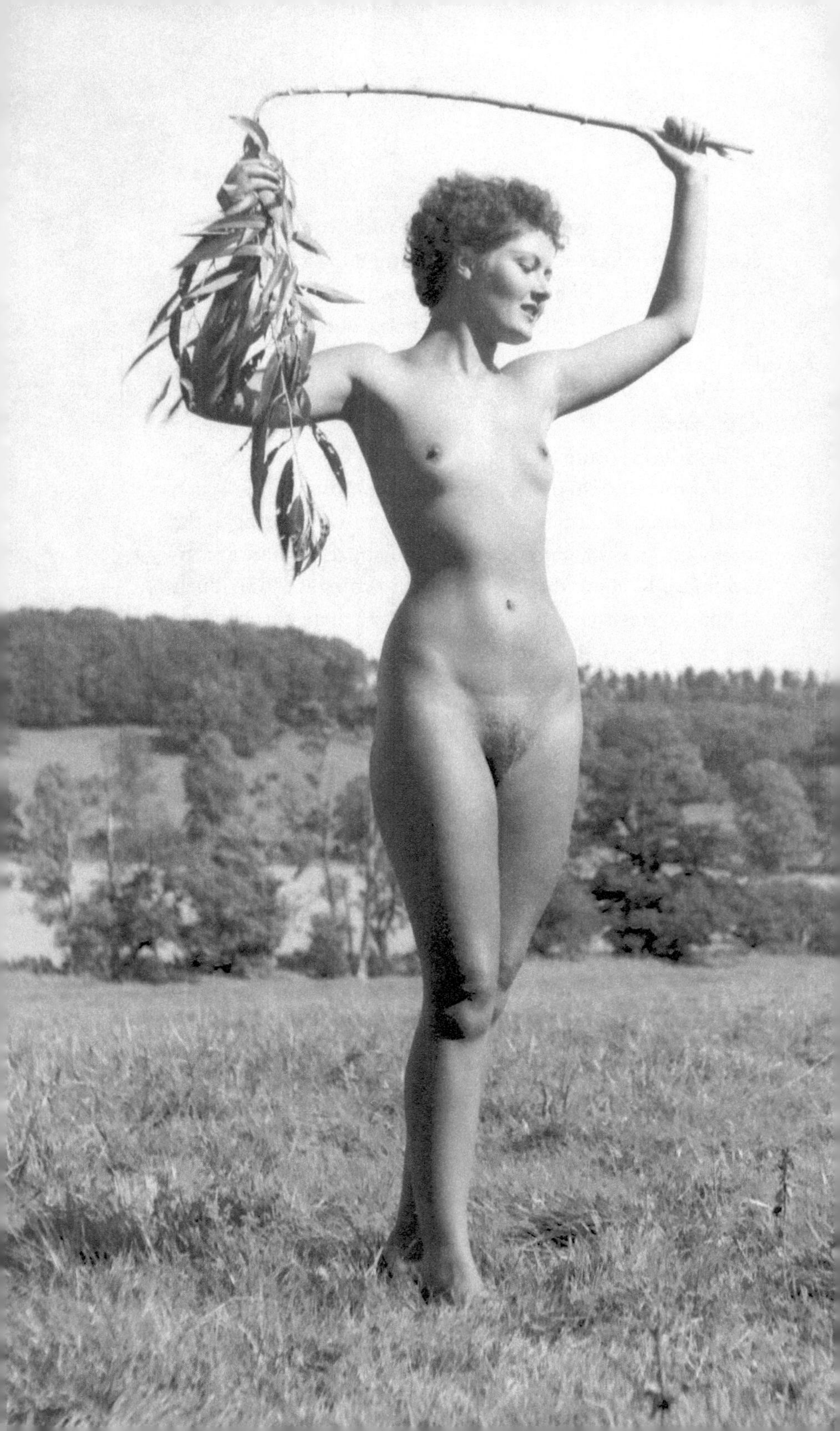

CHAPTER VIII

Has Nudism a Future?

A LOGICAL CONCLUSION to this book would seem to be a chapter on "The Future of Nudism." Other writers have used this title, but I am not going to use it because I am not sure that Nudism has a future. All revolutionary movements depend, in the long run, upon public opinion, and this is a very difficult thing to estimate in advance. At one time many people thought the cinema was just a passing craze and that roller-skating rinks would rank permanently among our social amenities. Time has proved them to be wrong. I believe that the practice of Nudism, as described in the previous chapters of this book, is such a sane and practical contribution to human health and happiness that it should become general and permanent. It has been stigmatised by some critics as a form of decadence. "Back to Nature means back to savagery," and so on; but this is a rather stupid and ill-informed view. There is no reason why we should not take advantage of scientific discoveries and inventions without relinquishing our rights to enjoy our lives in a simple and healthy manner. Nostrums and quack medicines are a poor compensation for the natural health which plain, wholesome foods, fresh air and exercise ensure. The types of men and women which are attracted by Nudism are by no means

---

Left: *Meadow Muse.*

those of ignorant, unthinking savagery; they usually are quite
the reverse and represent rather the intellectual type of progress which is prepared to revive truths and principles which
have become forgotten or obscured in the rush and turmoil
of modern times. It may be that the hectic conditions of to-
day call for a drastic reconsideration of such principles and
the establishment of salutary changes such as are offered by
Nudist philosophy, although I should hesitate to make such
an assertion. Other critics have claimed that Nudism is "the
fad of a moment" and point out that though the movement
originated in Germany and grew with mushroom-like ra-
pidity, it has since been repudiated in that country. This is
quite untrue. As I have explained in an earlier chapter, the
movement came into being under Socialist auspices and, in
Germany, was tainted by a political bias which brought it
under the ban of Mr. Hitler when he attained power. But
it was not Nudism itself to which he objected and he made
no attempt to interfere with purely private and non-political
Nudist centres, which are as flourishing to-day as they were
before the advent of the Nazi regime.

Of course, we have jokes about Nudists and Nudism. We
made fun of the idea that women should be allowed to ride
bicycles, that "mixed bathing" should be tolerated, and that
women should have votes. Yet all these things have come about
and come to stay. Personally, I think simple, clean jokes about
Nudism are quite harmless. and likely to help the movement
forward rather than otherwise. Think of all the jokes made
about the Ford car; the more ridicule it suffered, the more
other manufacturers became inspired to imitate the methods
of its inventor. I have mentioned "mixed bathing," and I can

remember the time when this was regarded with less tolerance amongst the general public than Nudism is to-day. As a small boy I used to bathe with my brother and male friends and relatives at one end of the beach while my sisters bathed at the other end, a mile or so away. When it became possible (thanks to the broadening of public opinion) for us all to bathe together, I felt a thrill as of something very daring, although I was completely at a loss to account for it. Certainly we boys learnt very little more about the female form, for the cumbersome, baggy costumes worn by ladies in those days made them look as shapeless as a sack of potatoes. It was a long time after mixed bathing in the sea was accepted before mixed bathing in swimming baths was permitted—somewhat of a parallel to the present feeling regarding outdoor Nudism and indoor Nudism.

If we agree with the axiom that "history repeats itself," it seems reasonable to suppose that Nudism is as likely to be accepted generally as mixed bathing and rational costumes. I see no reason why progressive seaside authorities should not set apart suitable coves or small bays for those who wish to bathe without costumes. Perhaps, at first, there might be separate sections for either sex, since the greatest objection seems to be the danger of observing the nudity of the opposite sex; but this prejudice would doubtless soon be outgrown. These special bathing beaches would, however, have to be segregated because there is a great deal of difference between the association of genuine Nudists and promiscuous exposure to the general public.

Then we might have "sun-bathing enclosures" in some of our public parks (as was the case in Germany) where those with

Nudist proclivities could divest themselves of their clothing and enjoy the sun and air without offence to those holding different views. These would provide accommodation for men and women who, for one reason or other, were unable to join regular clubs or for members of such clubs when far away from their own districts. It is not inconceivable that the time may come when a Government official will achieve fame and popularity by establishing such centres, as Mr. George Lansbury did when, as First Commissioner of Works, he provided the "Lansbury Lido" on the Serpentine in Hyde Park. In addition to Nudist bathing beaches at seaside resorts, the proprietors of hotels and boarding-houses may feature "sun-bathing enclosures" and bathing pools. Indeed, there are quite a few doing this already and, from what I have heard, they are extraordinarily well patronised. I have several friends who have spent most enjoyable holidays at such places and receive first-hand evidence of their growing importance. I believe, too, that the medical profession will support the movement to an even greater extent than at present.

There are, undoubtedly, a great many well-known medical men who are adherents of Nudism who, for professional and material reasons, are reluctant to make their opinions public. I think this is a great pity even though, at present, it may be considered unavoidable. I am a very humble person, but when I have told friends that I am writing on Nudism, I have been asked: "But, of course, you do not write under your own name?" Obviously, if I believed that such writing was in any way shameful I should not pursue it; but since I believe wholeheartedly in what I write, I feel it would be cowardly and insincere to use a pseudonym. I have not the least objection to anyone knowing I am a Nudist and that I and my wife and family enjoy healthy exercise and interesting companionship at a Nudist camp. I have often felt that the future of Nudism is very much dependent upon its frank acknowledgment. I have known many cases in which adverse critics have agreed that it cannot be very wrong when they know that I, or other people of whose respectability they are completely satisfied, practise it. If only the public at large was openly informed that certain well-known people are enthusiastic adherents of the movement, I am sure popular opinion would be greatly influenced. Unfortunately, popular opinion is like that. The knowledge that certain high dignitaries of the established Church, to say nothing of large numbers of Nonconformist ministers, approve of and practise Nudism, would do more to convince the doubters than any reasoned argument. And I think this will come.

But, as I said at the beginning of this chapter, I am not sure that Nudism has a "future" in the wide sense of the word. In the early stages of a movement there are always enthusiasts, and even martyrs, who will make sacrifices for it; but to become general and popular it must be made easy. If the pioneers are successful in breaking down prejudices and providing satis-factory opportunities for the general public to participate, they will be generously supported. Upon them, however, the brunt of the battle must fall, and if they relax their efforts and enthusiasm they will gradually fade into oblivion.

Nurse Cavell said: "Patriotism is not enough!"And it is not enough that Nudism should be carried on in isolated groups under the cloak of secrecy. I do not mean that Nudists should do anything rash or provocative. Stupid individuals who wish to show their courage and enthusiasm by challenging the law and exposing themselves in public are no friends of the movement. They merely lend colour to the criticisms levelled against it. Frankness and commonsense talks among friends will prove much more helpful. If you are a Nudist, do your best to make the people with whom you are in contact respect both your morals and your judgment and they will, in time, learn to respect Nudism through you.

Nudism is a principle which to be "understanded of the multitude" must be presented in a concrete and attractive form. Publicity and propaganda in its behalf needs to be conducted with skill and restraint since for its adoption many ingrained prejudices must first be abolished. The practice of some clubs to refuse inspection of their premises by potential members until a subscription has been paid is, in my opinion, a great mistake. Let members bring their friends to see what enjoyable times they may have by joining and judge for themselves the kind of people they will meet. The successful progress of clubs which grant such permission to properly accredited applicants is proof of the soundness of such a policy.

The future of Nudism, then, depends largely upon Nudists themselves. The leaders have it in their hands to build upon rock rather than sand, and if the existing fraternity and co-operation can be broadened Nudism can hope for a prosperous future. Once the general public learn of the improved health and mental outlook which come from Nudism it may become almost universal; but a few injudicious actions can easily destroy the fabric already built up. As a sincere well-wisher my advice to Nudists is to use their utmost endeavours to avoid antagonising non-Nudists, to prove by their own example that

Nudism is a beneficial influence. The rest may be left to the commonsense and honesty of the great general public whose word must decide the question as to whether Nudism has a "future" or not.

The End

WOLFBAIT
UNDER THE COUNTER CULTURE

ALSO AVAILABLE

Cinema au Naturel
A history of nudist film.

Miniten: Rules of the Game
Invented in the 1930s, Miniten is
a tennis-like game played by naturists.

Naked as Nature Intended
The epic tale of a nudist picture by Pamela Green, with
photographs by Douglas "Dambuster" Webb, DFM.

The Naked Truth About Harrison Marks
The notorious biography by Franklyn Wood.

Past Masters of the Nude
An illustrated bibliography of nude photography books
published in England from 1896 to 1960.

Slide Show
A luscious look at the photographic
slides of Harrison Marks.

X-ray Specs and Other Vintage Ads
A unique treasure chest of vintage advertising,
full of tease and prurient silliness.

Doing Rude Things
The history of the British sex film.

THE STEPHEN GLASS COLLECTION

Amazons of Yesteryear
A rare, action-packed collection of images of wrestling
women of the 1940s and 1950s.

Beauty Off-Duty
Relaxed, everyday moments caught on camera.

Naked in the Menagerie
A playful look at Eve accompanied by her animal friends.

Nudist Camp Follies — volumes 1 and 2
An intimate look at the natural
and free atmosphere in Sun Clubs.

Nymphs and Naiads
Beauty unadorned and outdoors.

Poise and Pose
A magnificent series of photographs
of female beauty taken in the studio.

THE EVA GRANT COLLECTION

The Glamour Camera of Eva Grant

A short biography of Eva Grant, one of the world's
foremost female figure photographers of the 1950s
and 1960s, accompanied by a selection of some
of her most enticing work.

Line and Form

A nostalgic review of Eva Grant's glamour
magazine of the 1950s.

Glamour Model Revue

Featuring June Palmer, Paula Page and Tina Madison.

THE WILLIAM WELBY COLLECTION

Naked and Unashamed:
Nudism from Six Points of View

William Welby's initial impressions of nudism.

The Naked Truth about Nudism

William Welby gets to bare all in this firsthand
exploration of British Naturism.

It's Only Natural: The Philosophy of Nudism

William Welby's musings on getting back to nature
and the tyranny of fashion.

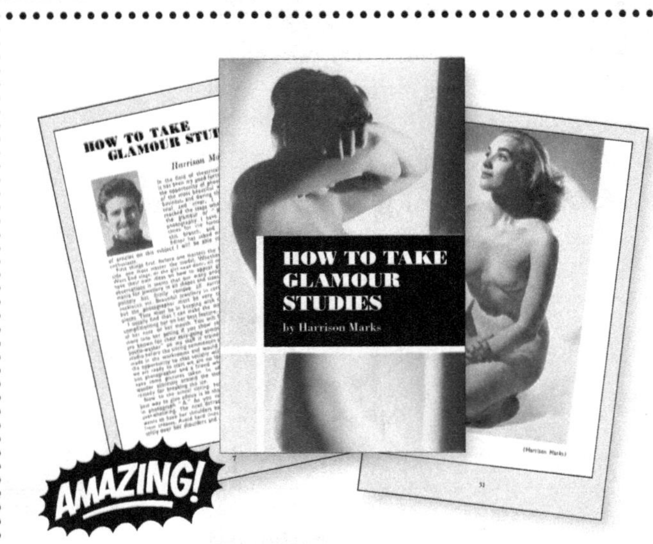

HOW TO TAKE GLAMOUR STUDIES
by Harrison Marks
(Harrison Marks)